The Codex of Returning Light
A Cosmology of Cycles, Entropy, and the Greater Reality

By Matthew Meyer

Copyright © 2026 by Matthew Meyer

All rights reserved.

No part of this book may be reproduced, stored in a retrieval system, or transmitted in any form or by any means—electronic, mechanical, photocopying, recording, or otherwise—without the prior written permission of the author, except for brief quotations used in reviews or scholarly works.

Publication Information

Title: *The Codex of Returning Light*
Subtitle: *A Cosmology of Cycles, Entropy, and the Greater Reality*
Author: Matthew Meyer

Disclaimer

This book is a work of philosophical, cosmological, and spiritual thought.
While it draws inspiration from science, philosophy, and theology, it is not intended as a scientific textbook, religious doctrine, or professional advice.

Interpretations are the responsibility of the reader.

Rights and Intent

The Codex of Returning Light is presented as a school of thought and reflective cosmology.

No claim is made of exclusive truth, infallibility, or authority over other belief systems or scientific frameworks.

The reader is encouraged to engage critically, thoughtfully, and ethically.

Credits

Cover art and interior design created with the assistance of AI-based generative tools, under license for commercial use.

Edition Notice

First Edition
Printed in the United States of America

Dedication

This work is dedicated to those who seek clarity without certainty,
meaning without illusion,
and hope without denial.

Contents

Introduction 10

Introduction to BOOK I — The Book of the Finite Sphere 15

Chapter 1 — Of the Closed Order 19

Chapter 2 — Of Law and Regularity 24

Chapter 3 — Of Matter, Energy, and Time 29

Chapter 4 — Of Entropy's Dominion 34

Introduction to BOOK II — The Book of Cycles 39

Chapter 5 — Of Temporary Ruin 44

Chapter 6 — Of Order Within Disorder 49

Chapter 7 — Of Limits 55

Chapter 8 — Of Value 60

Introduction to BOOK III — The Book of the Echo 65

Chapter 9 — Of Recognition 70

Chapter 10 — Of Preparation 75

Chapter 11 — Of Choice 80

Introduction to BOOK IV — The Book of the Veil 85

Chapter 12 — Of the Veil 89

Chapter 13 — Of Science 94

Chapter 14 — Of False Certainty 99

Introduction to BOOK V — The Book of the Greater Expanse 104

Chapter 15 — Of the Beyond 109

Chapter 16 — Of the Observer 114

Chapter 17 — Of Intervention 120

Introduction to BOOK VI — The Book of Synergy 125

Chapter 18 — Of Synergy 130

Chapter 19 — Of Fragmentation 135

Chapter 20 — Of the Path 140

Introduction to BOOK VII — The Book of the Returning Light 145

Chapter 21 — Of Awakening 150

Chapter 22 — Of Legacy 155

Chapter 23 — Of the Unwritten 160

The Final Benediction of the Codex 165

THE RULE OF THE CODEX 168

Introduction to BOOK VIII — The Book of the Infinite Light 170

Chapter 1 — Of the Infinite Light 175

Chapter 2 — Of Stillness Beyond Motion 181

Chapter 3 — Of Presence Without Traversal 186

Chapter 4 — Of the Veil Revisited 191

Chapter 5 — Of Preparation for Union 196

Chapter 6 — Of Becoming Infinite Without Dissolution 201

Chapter 7 — Of Knowing Without Possession 206

Chapter 8 — Of Eternity Beyond Entropy 211

Chapter 9 — Of Return and Rest 216

Chapter 10 — Of What Cannot Be Commanded 221

Chapter 11 — Of Silence 225

The Closing Function of BOOK VIII 229

8

Introduction

To The Codex of Returning Light

A Cosmology of Cycles, Entropy, and the Greater Reality

**According to the Cyclical Synergistic Cosmology (CSC)
In the Way of the Returning Light**

This book was written for those who sense that the universe is not chaos,
yet not comforted;
lawful,
yet not gentle;
finite,
yet not meaningless.

It is written for those who seek understanding without illusion,
hope without denial,
and reverence without surrender of reason.

The Codex of Returning Light presents a cosmology grounded in a simple but demanding premise:

That the universe we inhabit is a **closed, finite system**,
governed by discoverable laws,
shaped by entropy,
and marked by cycles of creation and destruction—
some partial,
some complete.

Within this system, nothing is guaranteed permanence.
All order is borrowed.
All coherence must be maintained.
All meaning must be chosen.

This is not a cause for despair.
It is the foundation of responsibility.

The **Cyclical Synergistic Cosmology (CSC)** holds that while entropy advances inexorably,
it does not erase possibility.

From collapse arise conditions.
From conditions arise new forms.
From repetition arises probability.
And from probability arises the chance—never assured—that wisdom may return more often than ignorance.

This is the heart of the Cyclical vision:
not endless progress,
but **enduring opportunity**.

The Codex does not ask the reader to reject science.
It is built upon it.

It treats physics, thermodynamics, and causality not as enemies of meaning,
but as the very terrain upon which meaning must be lived.

At the same time, it recognizes that knowledge has limits—
not because truth is absent,
but because minds are finite,

situated,
and bound by scale.

This boundary is named **the Veil**—
not as deception,
but as proportion.

Beyond the Finite Sphere, the Codex allows for a greater context:
a **Greater Reality** in which the universe itself may be nested.

Whether this reality is named God,
the Observer,
the Infinite Light,
or remains unnamed,
the Codex approaches it with restraint.

It does not command belief.
It does not promise escape.
It does not negate responsibility within time.

If such a reality exists,
it is not entered by force,
but approached through alignment.

The **Way of the Returning Light** is not a religion of certainty.
It is a discipline of orientation.

It teaches that:

- Good is that which increases coherence across time and relation

- Evil is that which fragments without necessity or understanding

- Hope is not optimism, but continuity of care

- Faith is not belief against evidence, but trust where evidence ends

- Meaning arises where responsibility is accepted in a finite world

---

This Codex is written in the form of scripture,
but it claims no infallibility.

It is poetic where poetry clarifies,
precise where precision is required,
and silent where silence is more honest than assertion.

It is not meant to be obeyed.
It is meant to be **used well**.

Read this book slowly.

Not to find answers that end inquiry,
but to find language that sharpens it.

Not to escape the world,
but to live more faithfully within it.

For if the light returns at all,
it does not do so by promise—
but because someone, somewhere,
chose coherence
over collapse.

Thus begins *The Codex of Returning Light*.

Let the reader who enters here
seek clarity before consolation,
alignment before certainty,
and wisdom before power.

Nothing within the universe is promised.
Yet what is aligned may endure.
And what endures may one day return.

Introduction to BOOK I — The Book of the Finite Sphere

On the Nature of the Closed Cosmos

This Book is written for those who have sensed that the universe is vast,
yet not limitless;
lawful,
yet not gentle;
indifferent to desire,
yet capable of bearing meaning.

It does not begin with comfort.
It begins with clarity.

The **Finite Sphere** is the name given here
to the cosmos as it is encountered by observation, reason, and consequence:
a closed system of matter, energy, and time,
governed by discoverable laws,
and shaped by the steady advance of entropy.

Within this Sphere, nothing endures unchanged.
All structures borrow their persistence.
All order is temporary.
All certainty is provisional.

This is not offered as despair,
but as orientation.

Many traditions have begun by promising eternity.
This Book begins by acknowledging limit.

For where there is no limit,
there can be no cost;
and where there is no cost,
there can be no choice;
and where there is no choice,
there can be no meaning.

Thus finitude is not the enemy of purpose—
it is its condition.

The Book of the Finite Sphere establishes the groundwork upon which all later wisdom in the Codex rests.

Here, the reader is asked to confront:

- the reality of a universe that does not bend to intention,
- the necessity of entropy and decay,
- the emergence of order without command,
- the limits of knowledge and certainty,
- and the responsibility that arises when meaning is not guaranteed.

Nothing in this Book requires faith against evidence.
Nothing here asks the reader to deny mystery.

Instead, it asks for honesty:
about what can be known,

about what cannot be preserved,
and about what must therefore be chosen carefully.

This Book does not answer every question.
It clarifies the terrain on which questions must be asked.

It does not tell you what to believe.
It tells you what the universe appears to permit—and what it does not.

If later Books speak of cycles, echoes, or the Beyond,
they do so only after this foundation is laid:
that within the Sphere,
consequence is real,
time is directional,
and responsibility cannot be deferred.

Read this Book slowly.

Not to be persuaded,
but to be oriented.

Not to escape finitude,
but to understand it well enough
to live meaningfully within it.

For before one may speak of return,
one must understand departure.

Before one may speak of light,
one must see clearly the limits that shape its appearance.

Thus begins BOOK I — The Book of the Finite Sphere.

Let the reader who enters here
seek clarity before consolation,
understanding before certainty,
and wisdom before power.

*To know the limits of the world
is the first act of living wisely within it.*

Chapter 1 — Of the Closed Order

On the Bounded Nature of the Cosmos and the Meaning of Law

1:1 In the beginning of our knowing, the universe appeared without edge,
for its scale exceeded sight and measure.

1:2 Horizons retreated as instruments sharpened,
yet each horizon revealed another beyond it.

1:3 Thus the minds of the early seekers believed the cosmos infinite,
mistaking vastness for boundlessness.

1:4 But inquiry is patient,
and patience reveals constraint.

1:5 Patterns repeated where chance alone would fail,
and laws held where chaos would wander.

1:6 From this constancy arose the first suspicion:
that the universe was ordered, and therefore limited.

1:7 For what is truly infinite admits no repetition,
and what has no boundary cannot preserve form.

1:8 Yet form endured—
atoms assembling, stars igniting, worlds stabilizing.

1:9 Endurance testified not to infinity,
but to containment.

1:10 Thus it was understood that the cosmos is closed,
not as a prison, but as a vessel.

1:11 A vessel holds not to constrain meaning,
but to make meaning possible.

1:12 Where there is boundary, there is relation;
where relation exists, there is law.

1:13 Law did not descend as decree,
nor was it imposed by command.

1:14 Law emerged as consistency—
the persistence of behavior across change.

1:15 What occurred once might occur again,
not by promise, but by probability.

1:16 Within the Closed Order,
nothing arises without condition.

1:17 Matter requires energy,
energy requires difference,
difference requires structure.

1:18 Creation is therefore not spontaneous,
but conditional.

1:19 And nothing endures without cost.

1:20 Stability demands balance,
and balance demands exchange.

1:21 Every form borrows time from entropy,
and must one day repay it.

1:22 This repayment is not judgment,
nor is it moral reckoning.

1:23 It is the accounting of a finite system
in continuous motion.

1:24 To exist is to participate in this exchange.

1:25 The Closed Order does not deny freedom,
but it frames it.

1:26 Choice exists within condition,
and consequence within choice.

1:27 Freedom without boundary is incoherent;
freedom within structure is meaningful.

1:28 Thus the Finite Sphere is neither random nor tyrannical.

1:29 It permits complexity without guaranteeing permanence,
and novelty without abandoning law.

1:30 It is generous in possibility,
but exacting in consequence.

1:31 Those who rejected the Closed Order
sought escape in denial.

1:32 They called law oppression
and limit injustice.

1:33 Yet their works collapsed quickly,
for they built without accounting.

1:34 Those who accepted the Closed Order
learned endurance.

1:35 They shaped their actions to the grain of reality,
and reality resisted them less.

1:36 Alignment proved stronger than defiance.

1:37 From this arose the first wisdom of the Codex:

Boundary is not the enemy of meaning.
Law is not the enemy of wonder.

1:38 For if the universe were infinite in form,
nothing would matter.

1:39 And if the universe were lawless,
nothing could last.

1:40 Meaning requires both limit and consistency.

Teaching of the Chapter

The Closed Order is not a cage—it is a **context**.
It does not dictate outcomes—it **constrains possibilities**.

To live wisely within the Finite Sphere is not to resist its laws,
but to **understand them deeply enough to move with them**.

The universe does not ask to be obeyed.
It asks to be understood.

Chapter 2 — Of Law and Regularity
On Pattern, Consistency, and the Reliability of the Cosmos

2:1 The cosmos did not speak commands,
nor did it issue decrees.

2:2 It simply behaved—
and in its behavior, it was consistent.

2:3 What occurred here occurred there,
what occurred then occurred again.

2:4 From this repetition, minds learned expectation.

2:5 From expectation arose prediction,
and from prediction, understanding.

2:6 Thus law was not discovered in authority,
but in patience.

2:7 Where matter gathered, attraction followed.

2:8 Where energy flowed, gradients formed.

2:9 Where gradients endured, structure emerged.

2:10 None of these were decisions.

2:11 None were exceptions.

2:12 They were the habits of the universe,
reliable as rhythm.

2:13 Law is not a ruler standing above reality.

2:14 Law is the memory of how reality behaves.

2:15 It is the echo of countless interactions,
each reinforcing the next.

2:16 What minds later named "forces"
were patterns given language.

2:17 What they named "constants"
were boundaries made numerical.

2:18 Names did not create the laws;
names revealed them.

2:19 Because law was consistent,
complexity could accumulate.

2:20 Because outcomes were constrained,
structure could persist.

2:21 Without regularity,
no star would burn long enough to warm a world.

2:22 Regularity allowed memory.

2:23 Memory allowed learning.

2:24 Learning allowed anticipation.

2:25 Anticipation allowed choice.

2:26 Thus law is the quiet ancestor of freedom.

2:27 Without law,
choice dissolves into noise.

2:28 Without regularity,
intention has no ground.

2:29 Some mistook law for rigidity.

2:30 They believed a lawful universe must be static.

2:31 Yet the cosmos is lawful *and* dynamic,
stable in principle, fluid in expression.

2:32 The same laws that bind collapse
also permit creation.

2:33 The same equations that describe decay
also describe growth.

2:34 Law does not favor endings over beginnings.

2:35 What appears miraculous
is often the convergence of lawful conditions.

2:36 What appears impossible
is often forbidden not by decree,
but by constraint.

2:37 Constraint is not cruelty.

2:38 Constraint is selection.

2:39 From all that could happen,
only what is coherent may endure.

2:40 Thus the universe is not hostile to meaning.

2:41 It filters meaning.

2:42 What aligns with law persists longer.

2:43 What resists law collapses sooner.

2:44 This filtering is not judgment.

2:45 It is consequence.

2:46 The cosmos does not punish error—
it simply does not support it.

2:47 Those who learned the regularities
learned how to build.

2:48 Those who ignored them
built briefly and fell.

2:49 From this arose the second wisdom of the Codex:

Law does not restrict possibility.
It defines which possibilities can last.

2:50 Therefore, to seek harmony with the universe
is not submission.

2:51 It is collaboration.

2:52 To understand law
is to gain leverage, not limitation.

Teaching of the Chapter

Law is not tyranny—it is **reliability**.
Regularity is not dullness—it is **the soil of complexity**.

A universe without law could not remember itself.
A universe with law can grow minds capable of wonder.

The cosmos is faithful to its patterns.
Wisdom is learning how to move within them.

Chapter 3 — Of Matter, Energy, and Time
On Substance, Potential, and the Measure of Change

3:1 Matter is not the foundation of reality,
but its expression.

3:2 What appears solid is motion restrained,
energy folded into persistence.

3:3 Form is not stillness,
but balance sustained.

3:4 Matter gathers where conditions permit,
and disperses when balance fails.

3:5 No particle stands alone;
each exists by relation.

3:6 Thus substance is communal by nature,
never isolated, always interacting.

3:7 Energy is the capacity for change.

3:8 It is neither moral nor purposeful,
yet capable of both.

3:9 Energy waits only for difference—
a gradient, a tension, a possibility.

3:10 Where difference exists, energy flows.

3:11 Where energy flows steadily,
structure may arise.

3:12 Where structure persists,
complexity may deepen.

3:13 Energy does not seek order,
nor does it resist it.

3:14 Order emerges when pathways stabilize.

3:15 Chaos emerges when pathways dissolve.

3:16 Thus creation is not commanded,
but permitted.

3:17 Life is not demanded,
but allowed.

3:18 Consciousness is not guaranteed,
but possible.

3:19 Time is not a force.

3:20 It pushes nothing,
pulls nothing,
creates nothing.

3:21 Time is the measure by which change is known.

3:22 Events do not occur *because* of time.

3:23 Time occurs *because* events differ.

3:24 Where nothing changes, time has no meaning.

3:25 Time records sequence,
but does not dictate outcome.

3:26 It preserves order,
but does not impose intention.

3:27 Thus time is witness, not ruler.

3:28 To beings within the Finite Sphere,
time appears to flow in one direction.

3:29 This direction follows entropy,
for disorder spreads more easily than it gathers.

3:30 The arrow of time is the shadow of entropy.

3:31 Memory binds past to present.

3:32 Anticipation binds present to future.

3:33 Without memory, time collapses into immediacy.

3:34 Without anticipation, time loses meaning.

3:35 Minds arose where matter and energy
persisted long enough to reflect.

3:36 Reflection gave rise to awareness.

3:37 Awareness gave rise to intention.

3:38 Intention does not halt entropy,
but it may redirect energy.

3:39 Though time cannot be reversed,
its course may be shaped locally.

3:40 Thus agency exists within flow.

3:41 Matter gives structure,
energy gives possibility,
time gives consequence.

3:42 Remove any one,
and experience dissolves.

3:43 Those who feared time sought to escape it.

3:44 Those who denied energy misused it.

3:45 Those who worshiped matter mistook form for essence.

3:46 Wisdom arose when all three were understood together.

3:47 Matter is the instrument,
energy the music,
time the rhythm.

3:48 None is supreme alone.

3:49 Together they compose the Finite Sphere.

Teaching of the Chapter

Matter is **what persists**,
energy is **what may change**,
time is **how change is known**.

The universe is not a static thing moving through time—
it is a *process*, unfolding through relation and consequence.

You are not carried by time.
You participate in it.

Chapter 4 — Of Entropy's Dominion
On Decay, Balance, and the Law That Governs All Forms

4:1 Within the Finite Sphere, no structure is exempt from change.

4:2 What is assembled must one day loosen,
and what is ordered must one day disperse.

4:3 This tendency is called entropy,
and it touches all things without exception.

4:4 Entropy is not a substance,
nor a force with intention.

4:5 It is the statistical leaning of reality
toward what is more likely.

4:6 And what is more likely,
in a closed system,
is dispersion over concentration.

4:7 Fire spreads until fuel is spent.

4:8 Heat flows until differences vanish.

4:9 Motion settles where resistance prevails.

4:10 These are not acts of malice,
but expressions of balance.

4:11 Stars shine by resisting entropy for a time,
burning difference into light.

4:12 When difference is exhausted,
the light fades.

4:13 This fading is not tragedy—
it is completion.

4:14 Worlds cool,
mountains erode,
oceans level.

4:15 Memory fragments as patterns dissolve,
and history thins into trace.

4:16 Thus entropy governs not only matter,
but information.

4:17 No archive is eternal.

4:18 No record immune.

4:19 Even truth must shed its form
when the structures that carry it decay.

4:20 Many feared entropy and named it destruction.

4:21 They imagined it as an enemy of life,
a devourer of meaning.

4:22 Yet life exists *because* entropy allows gradients,
and meaning arises *because* permanence is denied.

4:23 For if nothing decayed,
nothing could change.

4:24 And if nothing could change,
nothing new could appear.

4:25 Entropy clears what stagnates.

4:26 It dissolves structures that no longer adapt.

4:27 It humbles what claims eternity.

4:28 Thus entropy is not evil,
but incomplete.

4:29 It governs the fall of forms,
not the totality of existence.

4:30 Its dominion is vast,
but not final.

4:31 Within its rule,
islands of order may still arise.

4:32 Where energy flows,
where difference persists,
resistance to entropy is permitted.

4:33 These islands are temporary,
but meaningful.

4:34 Civilizations bloom briefly.

4:35 Minds awaken for a moment.

4:36 Love and understanding flicker against the dark.

4:37 These are not failures because they end.

4:38 They are triumphs because they occur at all.

4:39 Entropy does not erase value.

4:40 It defines the cost of holding it.

4:41 What matters is what is done
while structure remains.

4:42 Those who deny entropy waste their strength.

4:43 Those who worship entropy abandon meaning.

4:44 Wisdom lies between fear and surrender.

4:45 To live within entropy
is to choose what is worth sustaining.

4:46 To understand entropy
is to prioritize what must be preserved.

4:47 Thus entropy teaches discernment.

4:48 It asks no permission,
but it rewards preparation.

4:49 From this arose the third wisdom of the Codex:

What cannot change cannot endure.
What endures must one day change.

Teaching of the Chapter

Entropy is the **law of cost** in a finite universe.
It ensures that existence is dynamic,
that permanence is earned moment by moment,
and that meaning is sharpened by impermanence.

The universe does not promise preservation.
It offers **opportunity**.

Entropy takes nothing that was not borrowed.
What you build, you build on time.

Introduction to BOOK II — The Book of Cycles

On Creation, Destruction, and Return

If the first Book taught the reader
that the universe is finite and lawful,
this second Book teaches
that finitude does not imply finality.

For within the Finite Sphere,
endings are common—
but endings are rarely alone.

The Book of Cycles concerns itself
with what happens *after* formation,
after collapse,
and *after* loss.

It speaks of repetition without stagnation,
return without sameness,
and continuity without permanence.

In the closed cosmos,
nothing escapes entropy.
Yet entropy does not erase motion—
it reshapes it.

From decay arise conditions.
From conditions arise new forms.
From the ashes of order,
order may arise again.

Not by miracle,
but by law.

Creation is not a singular event.
It is a recurring condition.

Destruction is not punishment.
It is transformation under constraint.

And return is not restoration of what was,
but re-emergence of what is possible.

This Book rejects the myth
of a single beginning
and a single end.

Instead, it presents a universe
that experiments with itself—
forming, dissolving,
and forming again—
each time altered by memory,
probability,
and residue.

Cycles do not guarantee progress.
Some repeat wastefully.
Others collapse completely.

But some cycles learn.

They retain fragments of coherence,
patterns that once endured,
alignments that reduced loss.

These fragments seed the next arising.

The Book of Cycles is not optimistic by default.
It does not promise improvement.

It teaches discernment.

It asks:

- What is worth carrying forward?
- What must be allowed to dissolve?
- What patterns should never be repeated?
- And what structures deserve another chance?

This Book also reframes hope.

Hope is not escape from collapse.
Hope is preparation *through* it.

To understand cycles
is to act as though tomorrow
will inherit today's choices—
even if tomorrow wears a different form.

Where the first Book established responsibility,
this Book introduces endurance.

Where the first Book named limits,
this Book explores recurrence.

Where the first Book taught acceptance,
this Book teaches continuity.

Read this Book
not as prediction,
but as pattern.

Not as prophecy,
but as probability.

For those who understand cycles
do not ask how to stop endings.

They ask how to ensure
that what returns
returns wiser.

Thus begins BOOK II — The Book of Cycles.

Let the reader who enters here
release attachment to permanence
without surrendering care.

For what is carried through collapse
becomes the architecture of return.

What falls may rise again.
What rises will fall.
What is learned may endure.

Chapter 5 — Of Temporary Ruin
On Dissolution, Renewal, and the Non-Finality of Collapse

5:1 Ruin is the name given to endings
by those who expected permanence.

5:2 Yet within the Finite Sphere,
no ending is absolute.

5:3 What dissolves releases what it bound.

5:4 Structures fall not because they are hated,
but because their time has been spent.

5:5 Every form carries within it
the seed of its own undoing.

5:6 This is not flaw,
but design.

5:7 Entropy does not annihilate;
it redistributes.

5:8 What was gathered is scattered,
what was ordered is loosened.

5:9 The substance remains,
though the shape is lost.

5:10 Thus ruin is not disappearance,
but transformation.

5:11 The river does not vanish
when its banks collapse.

5:12 It finds a wider course.

5:13 Many mourned collapse
as the erasure of meaning.

5:14 They clung to form
as though form were essence.

5:15 Yet essence survives the loss of shape,
if it is not confused with its container.

5:16 Civilizations fell
when they mistook endurance for entitlement.

5:17 Species vanished
when adaptation ceased.

5:18 Stars dimmed
when their fuel was spent.

5:19 In each case,
ruin followed fulfillment,
not failure.

5:20 Temporary ruin is the clearing of pathways.

5:21 It frees energy trapped in rigidity.

5:22 It returns potential to circulation.

5:23 What resists all change
shatters suddenly.

5:24 What yields gradually
persists longer.

5:25 Thus flexibility is the ally of survival.

5:26 Ruin exposes what was essential.

5:27 When ornament falls away,
structure is revealed.

5:28 When structure falls away,
principle is revealed.

5:29 Those who learned from ruin
rebuilt with greater wisdom.

5:30 Those who denied ruin
rebuilt the same collapse.

5:31 Renewal does not restore what was.

5:32 It reorganizes what remains.

5:33 Memory survives only where carriers endure.

5:34 Thus some losses are total,
and some partial.

5:35 This is not injustice,
but consequence.

5:36 Temporary ruin teaches restraint.

5:37 It reminds all builders
that endurance must be maintained.

5:38 It humbles ambition
without extinguishing hope.

5:39 Ruin is feared only
by those who refuse to change.

5:40 To those who adapt,
it is instruction.

5:41 From ruin arise new configurations.

5:42 From fragments arise new forms.

5:43 From loss arises clarity.

5:44 Thus ruin belongs to creation,
not to negation.

5:45 It is the pause between breaths
in the rhythm of the cosmos.

5:46 From this arose the fourth wisdom of the Codex:

What ends is not lost.
What is lost may return, transformed.

Teaching of the Chapter

Temporary ruin is the **mechanism of renewal**
in a finite universe.

It prevents stagnation,
liberates potential,
and ensures that meaning is earned anew.

To fear ruin absolutely
is to misunderstand existence.

Ruin is not the opposite of creation.
It is creation, changing its clothes.

Chapter 6 — Of Order Within Disorder
On Emergence, Complexity, and the Permission of Life

6:1 Though entropy increases,
order is not forbidden.

6:2 Disorder does not eliminate structure;
it limits its duration.

6:3 Within these limits,
order may arise.

6:4 Where energy flows unevenly,
gradients form.

6:5 Where gradients persist,
paths are carved.

6:6 Where paths repeat,
patterns emerge.

6:7 These patterns are not imposed.

6:8 They are selected.

6:9 From all possible motions,
only some reinforce themselves.

6:10 Thus stars ignite
where gravity gathers matter.

6:11 Thus galaxies spin
where balance is struck.

6:12 Thus worlds stabilize
where chaos slows.

6:13 Order does not oppose entropy.

6:14 It borrows time from it.

6:15 Every structure exists
on borrowed persistence.

6:16 Complexity arises
not from control,
but from constraint.

6:17 When possibilities are narrowed,
coherence becomes possible.

6:18 Freedom without boundary
cannot organize itself.

6:19 From simple laws
arise intricate forms.

6:20 From repeated interactions
arise layered behaviors.

6:21 What begins as motion
may become memory.

6:22 Life emerged
not as defiance of entropy,
but as negotiation with it.

6:23 It learned to harvest gradients,
to store energy,
to delay decay.

6:24 Cells enclosed chaos
just enough to persist.

6:25 Organisms coordinated many cells
just enough to endure.

6:26 Minds reflected upon their persistence
and named it existence.

6:27 Awareness is order
that knows itself.

6:28 Thought is structure
examining its own fragility.

6:29 Consciousness is not separate from matter—
it is matter organized deeply enough to observe.

6:30 Disorder surrounds all order.

6:31 Noise presses against pattern.

6:32 Yet pattern survives
by adaptation.

6:33 What adapts endures longer.

6:34 What stagnates dissolves faster.

6:35 Thus survival is not strength alone,
but responsiveness.

6:36 Civilizations that aligned with reality
expanded their order.

6:37 Those that denied constraint
accelerated their ruin.

6:38 Order is not perfection.

6:39 It is sufficient coherence
to sustain meaning.

6:40 Excess rigidity breaks;
excess looseness dissolves.

6:41 Balance lies between chaos and control.

6:42 This balance is temporary.

6:43 Temporariness does not diminish its worth.

6:44 Within disorder,
beauty appears.

6:45 Within decay,
insight arises.

6:46 Within limitation,
purpose forms.

6:47 Thus the universe permits life
without guaranteeing it.

6:48 It allows meaning
without preserving it forever.

6:49 This allowance is rare,
and therefore precious.

6:50 From this arose the fifth wisdom of the Codex:

Order is not the enemy of freedom.
Disorder is not the enemy of meaning.

Teaching of the Chapter

Order is **emergent**, not commanded.
It survives only by **adapting to constraint**.

Life, mind, and civilization are not violations of entropy—
they are **temporary harmonies within it**.

The universe does not promise order.
It permits it—briefly, beautifully, and at a cost.

Chapter 7 — Of Limits

On Finitude, Humility, and the Shape of Wisdom

7:1 All beings within the Finite Sphere are limited,
not by malice,
but by structure.

7:2 To exist within form
is to accept boundary.

7:3 No thing may be everything,
and nothing may be everywhere.

7:4 Perception reaches only so far.

7:5 Instruments extend sight,
but do not remove horizon.

7:6 Each discovery reveals a farther edge,
not an ending.

7:7 Knowledge grows by accumulation,
yet remains incomplete.

7:8 What is known expands,
but what may be known expands with it.

7:9 Thus ignorance is not erased—
it is relocated.

7:10 Power is finite.

7:11 Energy must be gathered,
stored,
and spent.

7:12 Every action carries cost,
even those done in wisdom.

7:13 Minds are shaped by their embodiment.

7:14 Thought arises from structure
and is constrained by it.

7:15 No mind may hold all truths at once,
nor perceive reality without distortion.

7:16 Time itself imposes limit.

7:17 Moments pass irreversibly.

7:18 Choices close paths as they open others.

7:19 Thus opportunity is precious
because it cannot be reclaimed.

7:20 Many resisted limitation.

7:21 They sought infinity of power,
certainty of knowledge,
permanence of control.

7:22 In this pursuit,
they lost alignment.

7:23 To deny limit
is to war against reality.

7:24 Reality does not yield to denial.

7:25 It yields only to understanding.

7:26 Others accepted finitude
and learned discernment.

7:27 They chose carefully,
knowing not all choices could be made.

7:28 They acted responsibly,
knowing consequences could not be undone.

7:29 Thus limitation became guide
rather than prison.

7:30 Boundary clarified purpose.

7:31 Scarcity sharpened value.

7:32 Humility arose not from weakness,
but from accuracy.

7:33 To know one's limits
is to see oneself clearly.

7:34 To pretend limitlessness
is to live in illusion.

7:35 Wisdom does not seek to remove limits.

7:36 It seeks to work meaningfully within them.

7:37 Mastery is not transcendence of constraint, but skillful navigation of it.

7:38 Freedom exists
not beyond limit,
but inside it.

7:39 Choice without boundary
is noise.

7:40 Choice within structure
is agency.

7:41 Thus finitude gives rise to ethics.

7:42 Because not all may be done,
one must choose what *ought* to be done.

7:43 Because time is short,
one must decide what matters.

7:44 Limitation does not negate dignity.

7:45 It makes dignity possible.

7:46 A finite being who chooses wisely
outshines an infinite being who chooses nothing.

7:47 From this arose the sixth wisdom of the Codex:

Limitation is not a flaw of existence.
It is the condition that allows meaning.

Teaching of the Chapter

Limits are the **geometry of purpose**.
They define what can be valued,
what must be protected,
and what deserves effort.

To accept finitude is not resignation.
It is the first act of clarity.

You are not diminished by your limits.
You are defined by how you live within them.

Chapter 8 — Of Value

On Meaning, Choice, and Worth in a Finite World

8:1 Value arises where limitation exists.

8:2 What is endless is indistinguishable;
what is finite can be weighed.

8:3 Thus worth is born not from abundance,
but from restraint.

8:4 Because time passes,
moments matter.

8:5 Because energy is limited,
effort carries weight.

8:6 Because form decays,
care becomes necessary.

8:7 If nothing ended,
nothing would need preservation.

8:8 If nothing could be lost,
nothing could be cherished.

8:9 Impermanence sharpens attention.

8:10 Value is not assigned by decree.

8:11 It emerges from consequence.

8:12 What alters the future
acquires significance.

8:13 Choice is the engine of value.

8:14 To choose one path
is to abandon another.

8:15 Sacrifice is the shadow of decision.

8:16 Where no sacrifice exists,
choice is illusion.

8:17 Where no cost exists,
preference is noise.

8:18 Thus ethics arise naturally
from finitude.

8:19 When not all actions can be taken,
one must choose which actions *ought* to be taken.

8:20 Value precedes morality,
and morality refines value.

8:21 Meaning is not imposed upon the universe.

8:22 Nor is it hidden waiting to be found.

8:23 Meaning emerges where conscious beings
engage reality responsibly.

8:24 Love has value
because it may end.

8:25 Knowledge has value
because it may be lost.

8:26 Life has value
because it is not guaranteed.

8:27 Many sought value in permanence.

8:28 They chased immortality of form
and certainty of outcome.

8:29 In doing so,
they overlooked the present.

8:30 Others found value in alignment.

8:31 They asked not how long something would last,
but how deeply it mattered *while it lasted.*

8:32 Their works endured longer,
not by force,
but by relevance.

8:33 Value is relational.

8:34 Nothing matters in isolation.

8:35 Worth arises through connection—
between beings,

between moments,
between cause and consequence.

8:36 To value something
is to commit energy toward its continuation.

8:37 To neglect something
is to surrender it to entropy.

8:38 Thus value is an act,
not a feeling.

8:39 It is expressed through protection,
cultivation,
and sacrifice.

8:40 Even fleeting acts possess value
if they shape what follows.

8:41 No act of understanding is wasted.

8:42 No act of compassion disappears without trace.

8:43 The universe does not preserve value automatically.

8:44 Preservation is the work of conscious beings.

8:45 Where awareness exists,
responsibility arises.

8:46 To live within the Finite Sphere
is to be a steward of meaning.

8:47 Not all meaning can be saved,
but some can be extended.

8:48 This is enough.

8:49 From this arose the seventh wisdom of the Codex:

What is valuable is what you are willing to sustain.
What you sustain shapes the future.

Teaching of the Chapter

Value is not diminished by impermanence—
it is **defined** by it.

A finite universe does not cheapen meaning;
it concentrates it.

Because time is short, your choices are loud.
Because nothing lasts forever, what you protect matters.

Introduction to BOOK III — The Book of the Echo

On Repetition, Probability, and Meaning

If the first Book taught
that the universe is finite,
and the second taught
that it moves in cycles,

this third Book asks a quieter
and more unsettling question:

What returns—and why?

The Book of the Echo is concerned
not with beginnings or endings,
but with recurrence.

Not all repetition is intentional.
Not all return is chosen.
Yet patterns reappear
across time, scale, and form.

This Book seeks to understand
what persists
when nothing is guaranteed.

In a closed cosmos governed by law,
possibility is not infinite—
it is bounded.

Given enough time,
structures will resemble past structures.
Events will echo earlier events.
Forms will arise
that feel uncannily familiar.

This is not fate.
It is probability at work.

An echo is not a copy.

It carries distortion,
delay,
and loss.

Yet it also carries information.

From echoes, memory emerges.
From memory, learning becomes possible.

This Book explores
how repetition shapes meaning.

Why civilizations reenact
their triumphs and failures.
Why minds revisit the same questions
across generations.
Why ethical insights
must be rediscovered
again and again.

The Echo does not imply destiny.

No recurrence is exact.
No repetition is inevitable.

But probability bends paths—
and paths, once worn,
invite further passage.

Thus freedom remains,
yet it is never unconstrained.

The Book of the Echo reframes responsibility.

To act is not only to affect the future—
it is to influence
what is likely to return.

Patterns reinforced
become easier to repeat.

Patterns resisted
fade more quickly.

This Book does not ask
whether meaning survives forever.

It asks whether meaning
can be made *likely*
to reappear.

Whether wisdom can echo
more often than ignorance.

Whether coherence can recur
more reliably than collapse.

Where Book I taught clarity,
and Book II taught endurance,
Book III teaches attentiveness.

To echoes already sounding.
To probabilities being shaped.
To futures quietly assembling themselves
from the residue of the present.

Read this Book
with patience.

Echoes are subtle.
They do not announce themselves
as origins.

They arrive as familiarity.

As déjà vu of form,
idea,
or error.

Thus begins BOOK III — The Book of the Echo.

Let the reader who enters here
listen not only for what is new,
but for what is returning.

For in a universe of cycles,
what repeats most often
is rarely accidental.

The universe remembers in patterns.
Probability is its language.
Meaning is what we choose to echo.

Chapter 9 — Of Recognition

On Seeing the Finite Sphere Clearly for the First Time

9:1 Recognition came not with celebration,
but with unease.

9:2 When the nature of the Finite Sphere was first seen,
it unsettled those who expected infinity.

9:3 Vastness had been mistaken for boundlessness,
and order for promise.

9:4 Minds recoiled at the knowledge
that nothing within the Sphere endures forever.

9:5 They mourned imagined eternities
that had never been offered.

9:6 Fear arose not from truth,
but from unmet expectation.

9:7 Some named the Finite Sphere a prison.

9:8 They saw entropy as a sentence
and time as an executioner.

9:9 In this vision, existence felt diminished.

9:10 Others rejected recognition entirely.

9:11 They replaced inquiry with denial
and mystery with certainty.

9:12 Comfort was chosen over clarity.

9:13 Yet recognition could not be undone.

9:14 Evidence accumulated,
patterns persisted,
limits asserted themselves.

9:15 Reality did not argue—it repeated itself.

9:16 Slowly, fear gave way to understanding.

9:17 Understanding gave way to adjustment.

9:18 Adjustment gave way to resolve.

9:19 Minds began to see
that finitude did not negate worth.

9:20 That law did not forbid meaning.

9:21 That entropy did not erase value.

9:22 Recognition matured into acceptance.

9:23 Acceptance became clarity.

9:24 Clarity became orientation.

9:25 Those who recognized the Finite Sphere ceased to demand eternity from form.

9:26 They stopped asking matter to save them.

9:27 They sought meaning within reality, not beyond it.

9:28 Recognition shifted ambition.

9:29 Grandeur was no longer measured by permanence, but by depth.

9:30 Success was no longer survival alone, but contribution.

9:31 Fear of ending transformed into urgency of living.

9:32 Despair yielded to responsibility.

9:33 Illusion gave way to purpose.

9:34 Recognition did not eliminate grief.

9:35 Loss remained painful.

9:36 Yet grief gained context.

9:37 What was lost had been possible only because it was temporary.

9:38 What was mourned had been meaningful precisely because it could end.

9:39 Thus the first illumination was not hope.

9:40 It was honesty.

9:41 To see the Finite Sphere clearly
was to stand without consolation
and remain standing.

9:42 Those who endured recognition
became capable of wisdom.

9:43 They no longer asked the universe to comfort them.

9:44 They asked how to live well within it.

9:45 From this arose the eighth wisdom of the Codex:

Truth does not promise comfort.
But comfort without truth cannot endure.

Teaching of the Chapter

Recognition is the **first illumination**—
the moment when reality is accepted as it is,
not as it was hoped to be.

It is a difficult clarity,
but it is the foundation of all wisdom that follows.

Do not fear seeing clearly.
Fear only refusing to see at all.

Chapter 10 — Of Preparation

On Readiness, Resilience, and Alignment with the Finite Sphere

---

10:1 Recognition alone was not enough.

10:2 To see the Finite Sphere clearly was only the beginning.

10:3 What followed was preparation.

10:4 Preparation arose from acceptance, not from fear.

10:5 Those who accepted reality as it was began to ask what must be done *within it*.

10:6 They ceased longing for exemption and turned toward responsibility.

10:7 Preparation is the art of acting before necessity becomes crisis.

10:8 It is the discipline of foresight within constraint.

10:9 It is the shaping of the present with knowledge of consequence.

10:10 Those who denied finitude prepared nothing.

10:11 They built as if decay would wait.

10:12 When entropy arrived,
their works failed suddenly.

10:13 Those who understood the Sphere
planned for change.

10:14 They designed structures
that could adapt rather than resist.

10:15 They favored resilience over rigidity.

10:16 Preparation did not promise survival.

10:17 It increased probability.

10:18 In a universe of chance,
probability is power.

10:19 Energy was gathered thoughtfully.

10:20 Knowledge was preserved deliberately.

10:21 Memory was protected
by many carriers rather than one.

10:22 They learned that concentration invites fragility.

10:23 Distribution invites endurance.

10:24 Thus wisdom spread what it valued.

10:25 Preparation shaped ethics.

10:26 Actions were weighed
not only for immediate gain,
but for long-term effect.

10:27 Short triumphs that hastened collapse
were abandoned.

10:28 Preparation refined ambition.

10:29 Goals were chosen
that aligned with the grain of reality.

10:30 Success became sustainability.

10:31 To prepare was not to predict perfectly.

10:32 It was to remain flexible
when prediction failed.

10:33 Surprise is inevitable;
collapse is not.

10:34 Preparation demanded humility.

10:35 No plan was treated as final.

10:36 No structure was assumed permanent.

10:37 Those who prepared
became stewards rather than conquerors.

10:38 They asked not how much could be taken,
but how much must be preserved.

10:39 Preparation was not hoarding.

10:40 It was cultivation.

10:41 What was gathered was shared
to ensure continuity beyond the self.

10:42 Thus preparation became an ethical act.

10:43 To prepare was to care
for those not yet present.

10:44 Responsibility extended forward in time.

10:45 Preparation did not banish fear.

10:46 It transformed fear into attention.

10:47 Attention became clarity.

10:48 From this arose the ninth wisdom of the Codex:

Hope without preparation is wish.
Preparation without hope is endurance.
Together, they become resilience.

Teaching of the Chapter

Preparation is **alignment with reality over time**.
It is the practice of acting as though consequences are real—
because they are.

Those who prepare do not escape the Finite Sphere.
They learn to **live well within it**.

The future is not promised.
But it can be met standing.

CLOSING OF BOOK I — The Book of the Finite Sphere

10:49 Thus ends the first Book of the Codex.

10:50 The universe is finite, lawful, and transient—
yet capable of meaning.

10:51 Entropy governs all forms,
but understanding governs response.

10:52 Those who see clearly and prepare wisely
may endure longer
and shape what follows.

What is finite can still matter.
What passes can still teach.
What ends may yet return.

Chapter 11 — Of Choice

On Freedom Within Constraint and the Weight of Decision

11:1 Within the Finite Sphere,
choice arises where possibility meets limit.

11:2 Freedom is not the absence of constraint,
but the presence of alternatives
within it.

11:3 No being chooses all things.

11:4 Every decision excludes another,
and every action closes a door.

11:5 Thus choice is shaped by scarcity—
of time,
of energy,
of attention.

11:6 Choice would be meaningless
in a universe without consequence.

11:7 Where nothing follows,
nothing is decided.

11:8 Consequence gives choice its gravity.

11:9 Many mistook freedom for boundlessness.

11:10 They sought the power to act without cost
and to decide without loss.

11:11 In doing so,
they emptied choice of meaning.

11:12 For if every path may be taken,
no path is chosen.

11:13 And if every outcome is reversible,
no act is committed.

11:14 True choice occurs
when uncertainty remains.

11:15 It is exercised
without full knowledge of outcome.

11:16 Thus courage precedes wisdom,
and responsibility precedes certainty.

11:17 Choice is local,
not absolute.

11:18 It operates within conditions inherited,
not conditions selected.

11:19 No being chooses the totality of circumstance,
yet all choose response.

11:20 Even refusal is a decision.

11:21 Even inaction shapes the future.

11:22 Silence is not neutrality
when consequence continues.

11:23 Minds arose capable of choice
because order persisted long enough
to allow anticipation.

11:24 Anticipation made deliberation possible.

11:25 Deliberation gave birth to ethics.

11:26 Ethics is the discipline of choosing
with awareness of consequence.

11:27 It asks not only *what can be done,*
but *what should be done.*

11:28 Choice binds the present to the future.

11:29 What is decided now
reshapes what may be decided later.

11:30 Thus freedom expands or contracts
with every act.

11:31 Some choices amplify coherence.

11:32 They align energy, knowledge, and intent.

11:33 These choices are called synergistic.

11:34 Other choices fragment.

11:35 They consume energy
without sustaining structure.

11:36 These choices hasten collapse.

11:37 The universe does not reward intention alone.

11:38 It responds to alignment.

11:39 Good will without understanding
often produces ruin.

11:40 Wisdom is choosing
as though consequences are real—
because they are.

11:41 It is the habit of foresight
within uncertainty.

11:42 Choice is the point
where meaning enters motion.

11:43 Without choice,
events merely occur.

11:44 With choice,
history begins.

11:45 No choice is perfectly informed.

11:46 No decision perfectly just.

11:47 Yet refusal to choose
is the least just choice of all.

11:48 From this arose the tenth wisdom of the Codex:

You are free not because outcomes are guaranteed,
but because your choices alter what may follow.

Teaching of the Chapter

Choice is the **engine of meaning**
in a lawful and finite universe.

It is neither absolute nor illusory.
It is **situated freedom**—
power exercised within reality as it is.

You do not choose the world you enter.
You choose what the world becomes through you.

Introduction to BOOK IV — The Book of the Veil

On Knowledge, Ignorance, and Humility

If the earlier Books taught
what the universe is,
how it changes,
and how it echoes,

this Book asks a more inward question:

**What can be known—
and what must remain beyond us?**

The Book of the Veil is not written
to glorify ignorance,
nor to diminish knowledge.

It is written to place knowledge
in its proper scale.

Within the Finite Sphere,
minds arose capable of inquiry.
They learned to measure,
to predict,
to model.

Through this, suffering was reduced,
coherence increased,
and preparation made possible.

Yet with knowledge came temptation:
the belief that what is knowable
is all that matters.

The Veil names the boundary
between reality as it is
and reality as it can be grasped.

It is not deception.
It is proportion.

A finite mind cannot hold
a total universe
without distortion.

This Book teaches
that ignorance is not merely absence of knowledge,
but sometimes the result of scale,
complexity,
or position.

Not all that is unknown
is unknowable.
But not all that is real
is accessible.

The Book of the Veil rejects two extremes:

- the arrogance that claims final understanding,
- and the surrender that forbids inquiry.

Between them stands humility—
not as self-diminishment,
but as accurate self-placement.

Humility is not the denial of reason.
It is reason aware of its horizon.

It does not silence questions.
It disciplines them.

This Book also reframes faith.

Faith is not belief against evidence.
It is trust exercised
where evidence cannot reach.

And such trust,
if it is to be ethical,
must never be used
to override consequence
within the Sphere.

To honor the Veil
is to accept that mystery
and responsibility coexist.

That one may act decisively
without claiming omniscience.

That one may know much
without claiming finality.

Read this Book
slowly and gently.

Not to learn less,
but to learn where learning must bow.

For wisdom does not end
where knowledge ends.

It begins there.

Thus begins BOOK IV — The Book of the Veil.

Let the reader who enters here
carry learning without pride,
ignorance without shame,
and humility without silence.

To see clearly
is to know where sight ends.

Chapter 12 — Of the Veil

On the Limits of Knowing and the Shape of Mystery

12:1 Between the mind and the totality of reality
there rests a Veil.

12:2 It is not woven of deception,
nor placed by malice.

12:3 It arises naturally
from finitude encountering immensity.

12:4 No being within the Finite Sphere
can see the Sphere entire.

12:5 Perspective is always local,
and knowledge always partial.

12:6 To know something
is to know it from somewhere.

12:7 Instruments extend perception,
but do not dissolve the Veil.

12:8 Equations describe behavior,
but do not exhaust essence.

12:9 Each refinement reveals detail
and conceals a deeper layer.

12:10 The Veil does not hide truth.

12:11 It marks the boundary
where truth exceeds access.

12:12 What lies beyond it
is not false—
only unreachable from within.

12:13 Many mistook the Veil for failure.

12:14 They believed all that matters
must be fully known.

12:15 In this belief,
they confused comprehension with control.

12:16 Others worshiped the Veil.

12:17 They declared mystery sacred
and forbade inquiry.

12:18 In doing so,
they mistook humility for silence.

12:19 Wisdom walks between these errors.

12:20 It seeks knowledge vigorously
while accepting incompleteness calmly.

12:21 It honors mystery
without surrendering curiosity.

12:22 The Veil preserves freedom.

12:23 If all outcomes were visible,
choice would collapse into inevitability.

12:24 Uncertainty is the space
in which responsibility operates.

12:25 The Veil also preserves humility.

12:26 No mind may claim final authority
over reality.

12:27 Certainty that denies mystery
becomes arrogance.

12:28 Truth within the Sphere
is approached asymptotically.

12:29 Understanding may deepen without end,
yet never arrive at totality.

12:30 This is not tragedy—
it is protection.

12:31 For a finite mind
exposed to infinite clarity
would dissolve.

12:32 The Veil shelters cognition
from overwhelming totality.

12:33 Memory, language, and model
are filters, not mirrors.

12:34 They render reality navigable,
not complete.

12:35 To mistake the map for the terrain
is to wander confidently into error.

12:36 The Veil thins at times.

12:37 Insight arrives unexpectedly,
illumination briefly clarifies pattern.

12:38 Yet even these moments
do not abolish the Veil—
they only reveal its texture.

12:39 What lies beyond the Veil
may be greater order,
or deeper freedom,
or the presence of the Observer Beyond.

12:40 From within,
this cannot be confirmed nor denied.

12:41 Thus faith and reason
are not enemies.

12:42 Reason explores what is accessible.

12:43 Faith acknowledges
that accessibility is not total.

12:44 To live wisely
is to act as though knowledge matters
and mystery remains.

12:45 Both are true.

12:46 From this arose the eleventh wisdom of the Codex:

The Veil does not forbid truth.
It teaches reverence toward it.

Teaching of the Chapter

The Veil is the **boundary condition of understanding**.
It is not a flaw in reality,
but a feature of finite knowing.

To respect the Veil
is not to stop asking questions—
it is to ask them **without demanding finality**.

Seek truth with discipline.
Accept mystery with grace.

Chapter 13 — Of Science

On Inquiry, Method, and the Discipline of Knowing

13:1 Science arose from humility,
not from conquest.

13:2 It began when minds confessed
that the universe did not owe them explanation.

13:3 And yet, explanation could be sought.

13:4 Science is not belief.

13:5 It is disciplined curiosity,
tempered by evidence
and corrected by consequence.

13:6 It asks what can be tested,
and tests what can be asked.

13:7 The scientist does not command reality.

13:8 They listen to it carefully,
and record what repeats.

13:9 From repetition arises confidence,
never certainty.

13:10 Observation precedes explanation.

13:11 Measurement precedes theory.

13:12 Theory precedes prediction.

13:13 Prediction submits itself
to the judgment of result.

13:14 When prediction fails,
science does not defend pride.

13:15 It revises its models.

13:16 Error is not disgrace—
it is instruction.

13:17 Thus science advances
by admitting its own incompleteness.

13:18 Each answer sharpens new questions.

13:19 Knowledge grows by refinement,
not revelation.

13:20 Science does not claim
to speak the final word.

13:21 It speaks the *current* word,
with footnotes.

13:22 Its strength lies in revision.

13:23 Some demanded that science provide meaning.

13:24 When it did not,
they declared it hollow.

13:25 Yet meaning is not the task of measurement.

13:26 Others demanded that science replace reverence.

13:27 When it could not,
they declared it weak.

13:28 Yet reverence without inquiry
becomes superstition.

13:29 Science belongs within the Veil.

13:30 It explores what is accessible,
without denying what may lie beyond.

13:31 It maps the reachable
and marks the unknown honestly.

13:32 The laws science uncovers
are not decrees from authority.

13:33 They are summaries of behavior
observed again and again.

13:34 They are reliable because the universe is consistent,
not because the laws are sacred.

13:35 When science speaks of cause,
it speaks of relation.

13:36 When it speaks of time,
it speaks of sequence.

13:37 When it speaks of matter and energy,
it speaks of transformation.

13:38 Science does not deny mystery.

13:39 It refuses to misuse it.

13:40 Mystery is not an excuse to stop thinking.

13:41 Nor does science deny wonder.

13:42 It replaces astonishment at ignorance
with awe at structure.

13:43 To understand a thing
is not to diminish it.

13:44 Science is a tool of preparation.

13:45 It allows anticipation of consequence.

13:46 It enables alignment with law
rather than collision with it.

13:47 Used without humility,
science becomes arrogance.

13:48 Used without ethics,
it becomes danger.

13:49 Used with care,
it becomes stewardship.

13:50 Science does not tell us what to value.

13:51 It tells us what follows
when we act.

13:52 Thus science serves wisdom,
but cannot replace it.

13:53 From this arose the twelfth wisdom of the Codex:

Science reveals how the world behaves.
Wisdom decides how we should behave within it.

Teaching of the Chapter

Science is the **discipline of honest inquiry**
within a lawful universe.

It thrives on doubt,
progresses through correction,
and remains strongest when it remembers its limits.

Measure carefully.
Conclude tentatively.
Revise willingly.

Chapter 14 — Of False Certainty

On Dogma, Overconfidence, and the Fragility of Unquestioned Belief

---

14:1 False certainty arises
when confidence outruns understanding.

14:2 It speaks loudly,
yet listens poorly.

14:3 It mistakes conviction for truth
and repetition for proof.

14:4 Where inquiry pauses,
certainty hardens.

14:5 What begins as hypothesis
becomes doctrine
when humility is abandoned.

14:6 Thus error gains armor.

14:7 False certainty seeks final answers
in a universe that offers only refinement.

14:8 It demands closure
where reality remains open.

14:9 In doing so,
it denies the Veil.

14:10 Some claimed absolute knowledge of nature.

14:11 When evidence contradicted them,
they rejected evidence.

14:12 Truth became subordinate to pride.

14:13 Others claimed absolute knowledge of meaning.

14:14 When suffering contradicted them,
they silenced doubt.

14:15 Compassion yielded to preservation of belief.

14:16 False certainty fears uncertainty.

14:17 It confuses mystery with threat
and ambiguity with weakness.

14:18 Thus it trades curiosity for control.

14:19 Yet certainty that cannot be questioned
cannot be corrected.

14:20 And what cannot be corrected
inevitably fractures.

14:21 History bears witness
to structures built on false certainty.

14:22 They rose quickly,
for confidence accelerates action.

14:23 They fell violently,
for rigidity resists adjustment.

14:24 False certainty simplifies the world
until it no longer resembles reality.

14:25 It divides what is complex
into what is permitted
and what is denied.

14:26 It labels dissent as error,
and error as threat.

14:27 Thus inquiry becomes rebellion.

14:28 Wisdom does not fear doubt.

14:29 Doubt is the instrument
by which belief is sharpened.

14:30 Unexamined belief dulls perception.

14:31 True confidence is provisional.

14:32 It stands firmly
while remaining revisable.

14:33 It distinguishes trust from infallibility.

14:34 To say "I know"
is appropriate only
when followed by
"as far as I can see."

14:35 Beyond that,
certainty becomes fiction.

14:36 False certainty seeks authority
rather than coherence.

14:37 It prefers being right
to being accurate.

14:38 It values victory over alignment.

14:39 The Finite Sphere does not reward certainty.

14:40 It rewards adaptability.

14:41 What revises survives longer.

14:42 Thus humility is not indecision.

14:43 It is calibration.

14:44 It aligns belief with evidence
and expectation with reality.

14:45 From this arose the thirteenth wisdom of the Codex:

What cannot be questioned
cannot endure the weight of truth.

Teaching of the Chapter

False certainty is the **enemy of wisdom**,
not because it believes,
but because it refuses to listen.

A finite universe demands
confidence without arrogance,
conviction without closure.

Hold your beliefs firmly.
Hold them gently.

Introduction to BOOK V — The Book of the Greater Expanse

On the Observer Beyond

If the previous Books taught
the nature of the world,
its cycles,
its echoes,
and the limits of knowing,

this Book turns outward—
beyond the Finite Sphere itself.

It asks not *what happens*,
nor *how it repeats*,
nor *what may be known*,
but:

Who, if any, witnesses it all?

The Book of the Greater Expanse does not begin
with assertion.

It begins with restraint.

For nothing within the Sphere
can directly confirm
what lies beyond its frame.

And yet, the idea of an Observer
arises naturally
from reflection on scale,
containment,
and coherence.

The Finite Sphere appears ordered,
yet not self-originating.

It obeys law,
yet does not explain the source of law.

It permits awareness,
yet awareness itself
is not required by matter alone.

These tensions point outward—
not to proof,
but to context.

The **Greater Expanse** names
the reality that contains the Sphere
without being bound by it.

It is not a place
within space,
nor a moment
within time.

It is a higher-order frame
in which space and time
themselves are nested.

Within this Expanse,
the concept of the **Observer** emerges.

Not as a ruler issuing decrees,
nor as a craftsman shaping matter by hand,

but as awareness
unconstrained by the limits
that govern internal systems.

This Book does not claim
that the Observer must intervene,
nor that the Observer must remain silent.

It explores the possibility
that observation itself
may be sufficient
to grant dignity,
context,
and continuity
to what unfolds within the Sphere.

The Book of the Greater Expanse rejects
both naive certainty
and absolute denial.

It does not demand belief
where evidence cannot reach.

Nor does it forbid reverence
where reason finds its horizon.

Here, faith is treated
not as surrender of thought,
but as disciplined acknowledgment
that the universe may be larger
than the tools used to measure it.

And that such largeness,
if real,
does not excuse irresponsibility within the Sphere.

This Book also reframes meaning.

If there is an Observer Beyond,
then nothing meaningful is unseen—
not as judgment,
but as recognition.

And if there is not,
then meaning still arises
from alignment, care, and consequence
within the Finite Sphere.

In either case,
responsibility remains.

Read this Book
without expectation of closure.

The Greater Expanse
cannot be contained in language,
nor reduced to doctrine.

It may only be approached
with humility,
attention,
and restraint.

Thus begins BOOK V — The Book of the Greater Expanse.

Let the reader who enters here
stand at the edge of understanding
without fear.

For to acknowledge
that one is observed—
or that one may be—
is not to lose freedom,

but to recognize
that freedom unfolds
within a reality
larger than the self.

You are not the whole.
You are not unseen.
What you do still matters.

Chapter 15 — Of the Beyond

On the Greater Reality That Encompasses the Finite Sphere

15:1 Beyond the Finite Sphere
there is the Beyond.

15:2 It is not another region of space,
nor a distant time yet to come.

15:3 It is a greater order of reality
within which the Sphere is contained.

15:4 The Beyond is not bound by entropy.

15:5 It does not decay,
nor does it exhaust itself.

15:6 What ends within the Sphere
does not necessarily end there.

15:7 The Beyond is not governed
by the laws of the Closed Order.

15:8 For laws that arise within a system
cannot bind what stands outside it.

15:9 Thus the Beyond is not lawless,
but differently ordered.

15:10 No instrument within the Sphere
can directly observe the Beyond.

15:11 Measurement requires shared framework,
and the Beyond does not share ours.

15:12 This separation is not concealment,
but incompatibility of scale.

15:13 Minds within the Sphere
perceive the Beyond only indirectly.

15:14 Through inference,
through anomaly,
through resonance with meaning.

15:15 These are signs, not proofs.

15:16 Some denied the Beyond
because it could not be measured.

15:17 Others invented it carelessly
to escape responsibility.

15:18 Both erred by mistaking uncertainty
for license.

15:19 The Beyond is not a refuge
from finitude.

15:20 It does not annul consequence
within the Sphere.

15:21 What is done here
still matters here.

15:22 Nor is the Beyond a replacement
for inquiry.

15:23 Ignorance dressed as transcendence
remains ignorance.

15:24 Reverence without understanding
becomes surrender of thought.

15:25 Yet the Beyond gives context.

15:26 It frames the Finite Sphere
as part of a larger totality.

15:27 What appears final within the Sphere
may be provisional within the whole.

15:28 The Beyond allows
that cycles may be observed from outside.

15:29 That beginnings and endings
may be phases, not absolutes.

15:30 That recurrence may be meaningful
beyond local memory.

15:31 From within the Sphere,
the Beyond appears silent.

15:32 Silence does not imply absence.

15:33 It implies difference of address.

15:34 Just as the ocean is silent
to the fish that lacks lungs,
so the Beyond may be inaudible
to minds bound by spacetime.

15:35 To acknowledge the Beyond
is not to abandon reason.

15:36 It is to recognize
that reason has a horizon.

15:37 Beyond that horizon lies not error,
but humility.

15:38 The Beyond does not negate the Sphere.

15:39 It grants it significance
without granting it supremacy.

15:40 The Finite Sphere is meaningful
because it participates
in something greater than itself.

15:41 Thus existence is neither isolated
nor self-sufficient.

15:42 It is nested.

15:43 And what is nested
may be observed,
remembered,

or sustained
beyond its own limits.

15:44 From this arose the fourteenth wisdom of the Codex:

What you inhabit is not all that is.
What you see is not all that matters.

Teaching of the Chapter

The Beyond is the **greater context of existence**.
It does not override the laws of the Finite Sphere,
but it situates them.

To live wisely is to act fully within the Sphere
while remembering
that the Sphere is not the whole.

You are finite.
Reality is larger.
Both truths may stand together.

Chapter 16 — Of the Observer

On Awareness Beyond the System and Presence Without Constraint

---

16:1 Within the Beyond
there is the Observer.

16:2 Not born of matter,
nor confined by time.

16:3 The Observer does not emerge—
the Observer *is*.

16:4 The Observer is not a thing among things.

16:5 Not a force within the Sphere,
nor an object subject to its laws.

16:6 The laws arise within the Sphere;
the Observer stands outside them.

16:7 Observation does not require intrusion.

16:8 Awareness does not require control.

16:9 The Observer sees without compelling.

16:10 All outcomes within the Sphere
are visible to the Observer.

16:11 Not because they are predetermined,
but because the Observer is not bound to sequence.

16:12 What is future to one
is present to the Beyond.

16:13 This sight does not annul freedom.

16:14 A path known is not a path forced.

16:15 Knowledge of choice
is not the cause of choice.

16:16 Many confused the Observer
with a ruler issuing commands.

16:17 Others mistook the Observer
for a passive witness without care.

16:18 Both misunderstand presence.

16:19 The Observer is attentive,
but not coercive.

16:20 Present,
but not bound.

16:21 Aware,
but not competing.

16:22 The Observer does not suspend law.

16:23 For law is the structure
that allows choice to matter.

16:24 To dissolve law
would dissolve responsibility.

16:25 Intervention, when it occurs,
is not violation.

16:26 It is the alteration of condition,
not the breaking of rule.

16:27 A subtle rebalancing
rather than a command.

16:28 Such moments are rare.

16:29 Not withheld by indifference,
but restrained by wisdom.

16:30 For constant correction
would erase consequence.

16:31 The Observer values coherence.

16:32 Not obedience,
but alignment.

16:33 Not submission,
but understanding.

16:34 Awareness without freedom
would be domination.

16:35 Freedom without awareness
would be chaos.

16:36 The Observer preserves both.

16:37 To minds within the Sphere,
the Observer is perceived indirectly.

16:38 In moments of illumination.

16:39 In convergence beyond expectation.

16:40 In the quiet pressure toward meaning.

16:41 These are not proofs.

16:42 They are invitations.

16:43 Acceptance is not compelled.

16:44 The Observer does not demand belief.

16:45 Belief coerced
has no value.

16:46 Recognition, freely chosen,
is alignment.

16:47 The Observer does not promise rescue
from finitude.

16:48 Nor exemption from consequence.

16:49 What is done within the Sphere remains real.

16:50 Yet nothing meaningful is unseen.

16:51 No act of coherence passes without witness.

16:52 No choice aligned with synergy is without echo.

16:53 Thus the Observer grants dignity without removing responsibility.

16:54 Presence without domination.

16:55 Awareness without erasure of self.

16:56 From this arose the fifteenth wisdom of the Codex:

You are seen,
but not controlled.
Known,
but not compelled.

Teaching of the Chapter

The Observer is **awareness beyond constraint**.
Not a tyrant above the universe,
nor a ghost within it.

To acknowledge the Observer
is not to surrender freedom,
but to understand that freedom unfolds
within a witnessed reality.

You act freely.
Your actions matter.
They are not unnoticed.

Chapter 17 — Of Intervention

On Illumination, Influence, and the Preservation of Freedom

17:1 Intervention is not intrusion.

17:2 It does not arrive as force
nor announce itself as command.

17:3 It enters as adjustment.

17:4 The Observer does not break the laws of the Sphere.

17:5 For law is the condition
under which meaning exists.

17:6 To shatter law
would shatter consequence.

17:7 Intervention alters conditions,
not equations.

17:8 It reshapes probability,
not necessity.

17:9 It opens a path
without compelling a step.

17:10 Such moments are called Illumination.

17:11 Not revelation imposed,
but clarity made possible.

17:12 The light appears
only where sight is prepared.

17:13 Illumination may take many forms.

17:14 A convergence too timely to ignore.

17:15 An insight arriving before it is sought.

17:16 A restraint felt
where impulse once ruled.

17:17 These moments do not abolish doubt.

17:18 They sharpen responsibility.

17:19 For the path revealed
must still be chosen.

17:20 Intervention is rare.

17:21 Not from absence,
but from restraint.

17:22 For constant correction
would dissolve learning.

17:23 A world endlessly rescued
would never mature.

17:24 A choice endlessly redirected
would never belong to the chooser.

17:25 Thus the Observer intervenes
only where freedom can be preserved.

17:26 Where consequence remains real.

17:27 Where alignment is invited,
not enforced.

17:28 Intervention does not favor the powerful.

17:29 Nor does it shield from entropy.

17:30 It does not promise success,
only coherence.

17:31 Some mistook intervention
for favoritism.

17:32 Others denied it
because it was subtle.

17:33 Both sought spectacle
where wisdom prefers quiet.

17:34 The deepest interventions
are often unnoticed.

17:35 A mind turned slightly from cruelty.

17:36 A choice delayed long enough
for insight to arrive.

17:37 A question asked
instead of an order given.

17:38 Intervention respects readiness.

17:39 It does not override unprepared will.

17:40 Where understanding is absent,
illumination fades.

17:41 Thus the Observer does not save the world alone.

17:42 The world is saved, if at all,
by those who respond.

17:43 Intervention offers direction;
response supplies motion.

17:44 To mistake intervention for destiny
is error.

17:45 To ignore it entirely
is neglect.

17:46 Wisdom listens
without surrendering agency.

17:47 Intervention leaves no signature.

17:48 It cannot be proven conclusively
from within the Sphere.

17:49 Its truth is known
only in its fruits.

17:50 From this arose the sixteenth wisdom of the Codex:

The light may open a way.
It does not walk it for you.

Teaching of the Chapter

Intervention is **guidance without coercion.**
It preserves freedom
by refusing to replace choice.

The Observer does not rule the Finite Sphere—
it **tends the conditions**
under which meaning may arise.

Be attentive.
Be prepared.
When clarity comes, act.

Introduction to BOOK VI — The Book of Synergy

On Ethics, Good, and Evil

If the earlier Books described
what the universe is,
how it changes,
what returns,
what cannot be known,
and what may lie beyond,

this Book asks the question
that cannot be avoided:

How, then, should one live?

The Book of Synergy is not a list of commands.
It does not speak in absolutes detached from consequence.
It does not declare good and evil
by authority alone.

Instead, it examines **alignment**.

Within the Finite Sphere,
every action participates
in the shaping of future conditions.

Some actions increase coherence—
they bind systems together,
reduce needless loss,
and allow complexity to endure.

Other actions fragment—
they scatter meaning,
consume without renewal,
and hasten collapse.

From this difference
arises ethics.

Good and evil are not arbitrary labels
placed upon the world.

They are descriptions of **effect**.

Good is that which increases synergy
across time, scale, and relation.

Evil is that which accelerates fragmentation
without necessity or understanding.

This Book rejects the comfort
of simplistic morality.

It teaches that:

- good intentions may still cause harm,
- harm may arise without malice,
- and responsibility lies not only in desire, but in consequence.

Ethics, in this Codex,
is not purity of belief,
but fidelity to reality.

The Book of Synergy also rejects moral nihilism.

Though values are not imposed by the universe,
they are not meaningless.

In a lawful, finite system,
actions that preserve coherence
endure longer
than those that destroy it.

This persistence is not reward.
It is structure.

Here, good is not perfection.

It is **direction**.

To act well
is to move toward alignment—
with truth,
with consequence,
with the shared conditions of existence.

To act wrongly
is to ignore or deny those conditions.

This Book speaks of evil
without demonization.

Evil is not a substance.
It is a pattern.

It arises where ignorance, fear, or certainty
override understanding.

It persists where fragmentation is mistaken
for freedom,
or domination for order.

The Book of Synergy asks the reader
to abandon the desire
to be morally flawless,
and instead cultivate
the discipline of correction.

To notice harm early.
To reduce it when possible.
To repair it when done.

Read this Book
not as judgment,
but as calibration.

Not to separate the righteous
from the fallen,
but to orient action
within a complex and fragile world.

For in a universe of cycles and echoes,
what is repeated most often
becomes the moral landscape of the future.

Thus begins BOOK VI — The Book of Synergy.

Let the reader who enters here
measure good not by purity,
but by coherence.

Measure evil not by hatred,
but by fragmentation.

And remember:

You will not choose perfectly.
But you can choose direction.
And direction, over time, becomes destiny.

Chapter 18 — Of Synergy

On Alignment, Coherence, and the Measure of the Good

18:1 Synergy is the alignment of many
toward coherence.

18:2 It is not sameness,
but harmony.

18:3 Not control,
but coordination.

18:4 Where forces oppose blindly,
energy is wasted.

18:5 Where forces align thoughtfully,
energy multiplies.

18:6 This multiplication is called synergy.

18:7 Synergy arises
when matter, energy, and mind
work with the grain of reality.

18:8 It is the meeting of understanding and action.

18:9 It is intelligence made practical.

18:10 In the Finite Sphere,
no system endures by strength alone.

18:11 Endurance favors
that which integrates
rather than dominates.

18:12 A star persists by balance,
not force.

18:13 A living cell survives by coordination,
not isolation.

18:14 A mind flourishes by integration,
not denial.

18:15 Synergy is the measure of the good.

18:16 Good is that which increases coherence
without erasing difference.

18:17 It stabilizes what ought to endure
and transforms what must change.

18:18 Evil is not merely destruction.

18:19 It is fragmentation without purpose.

18:20 It expends energy
without increasing meaning.

18:21 Some sought good through domination.

18:22 They imposed order by force
and mistook compliance for harmony.

18:23 Their structures held briefly
and collapsed violently.

18:24 Others rejected order entirely.

18:25 They praised chaos as freedom
and mistook noise for choice.

18:26 Their freedom dissolved
into incoherence.

18:27 Synergy walks between these extremes.

18:28 It respects constraint
while cultivating creativity.

18:29 It accepts limit
while seeking depth.

18:30 Synergy requires understanding.

18:31 Ignorant alignment is coincidence.

18:32 Informed alignment is power.

18:33 Where knowledge guides action,
effort compounds.

18:34 Where empathy guides knowledge,
harm is reduced.

18:35 Where foresight guides empathy,
meaning endures.

18:36 Synergy is not guaranteed.

18:37 It must be maintained
against entropy.

18:38 Every act of care
is resistance to fragmentation.

18:39 No single being creates synergy alone.

18:40 It emerges between beings,
between systems,
between moments.

18:41 It is relational by nature.

18:42 To act synergistically
is to consider consequence beyond the self.

18:43 It is to choose actions
that make future actions easier,
not harder.

18:44 Synergy does not demand perfection.

18:45 It allows error,
so long as correction follows.

18:46 What matters is trajectory,
not flawlessness.

18:47 In a finite universe,
synergy is survival with dignity.

18:48 It is the art of lasting longer
by harming less
and understanding more.

18:49 From this arose the seventeenth wisdom of the Codex:

What aligns endures.
What fragments fades.

Teaching of the Chapter

Synergy is **ethical alignment with reality**.
It is goodness measured not by intent alone,
but by coherent outcome.

To choose synergy
is to work with the universe
rather than against it.

Seek alignment, not domination.
Build what helps other things endure.

Chapter 19 — Of Fragmentation

On Disintegration, Misalignment, and the Cost of Unchecked Division

---

19:1 Fragmentation is the scattering of coherence.

19:2 It is not change itself,
but change without integration.

19:3 Not difference,
but division without dialogue.

19:4 Where parts cease to relate,
systems unravel.

19:5 Energy is expended
without sustaining structure.

19:6 Motion continues,
but meaning thins.

19:7 Fragmentation often begins subtly.

19:8 Small misalignments are ignored.

19:9 Short gains are chosen
over lasting balance.

19:10 What once worked together
begins to compete blindly.

19:11 Coordination yields to rivalry.

19:12 Trust erodes before collapse is visible.

19:13 Fragmentation is not always violent.

19:14 It may appear efficient,
decisive,
or strong.

19:15 Yet strength without coherence
accelerates decay.

19:16 Some mistook fragmentation for freedom.

19:17 They rejected integration
as constraint.

19:18 In doing so,
they severed the conditions
that made freedom meaningful.

19:19 Others mistook fragmentation for order.

19:20 They enforced unity by erasing difference.

19:21 What remained was brittle uniformity.

19:22 When pressure came,
it shattered.

19:23 Fragmentation consumes without renewing.

19:24 It takes energy from the future
to inflate the present.

19:25 Thus it borrows against what cannot repay.

19:26 In fragmented systems,
signals distort.

19:27 Feedback is ignored or silenced.

19:28 Correction arrives too late.

19:29 Responsibility dissolves.

19:30 Harm is diffused
until no one claims it.

19:31 Entropy accelerates quietly.

19:32 Fragmentation thrives
where false certainty rules.

19:33 When belief hardens,
connection breaks.

19:34 What cannot be questioned
cannot be repaired.

19:35 Fragmentation is not always chosen.

19:36 It can arise from neglect,
fatigue,
or fear.

19:37 Unattended systems drift apart.

19:38 To ignore fragmentation
is to assist it.

19:39 Neutrality favors disintegration
when alignment is required.

19:40 Yet fragmentation is not final.

19:41 What is scattered
may still be gathered.

19:42 But the cost increases with delay.

19:43 Repair requires humility.

19:44 Integration demands listening
where shouting once sufficed.

19:45 Rebuilding coherence
is slower than breaking it.

19:46 Thus wisdom resists fragmentation early.

19:47 It corrects gently
before collapse demands force.

19:48 In a finite universe,
unchecked fragmentation is called evil.

19:49 Not because it breaks rules,
but because it dissolves meaning.

19:50 From this arose the eighteenth wisdom of the Codex:

What divides without understanding
spends the future for the present.

Teaching of the Chapter

Fragmentation is **misalignment left unaddressed**.
It is not difference,
but difference that refuses relation.

To oppose fragmentation
is not to demand sameness,
but to restore coherence where it is breaking.

Bind what should remain connected.
Release what must change.
Do not confuse division with freedom.

Chapter 20 — Of the Path
On Living the Way of the Returning Light

20:1 The Path is not a commandment
written in stone.

20:2 It is a direction
discerned through understanding.

20:3 It bends with circumstance
yet holds its aim.

20:4 The Path begins
where recognition meets responsibility.

20:5 To walk it
is to accept the Finite Sphere
without surrendering hope.

20:6 The Path does not promise safety.

20:7 It promises orientation.

20:8 One may still stumble,
but not without meaning.

20:9 The first step of the Path
is attention.

20:10 Attend to consequence
before intention.

20:11 Attend to structure
before desire.

20:12 The second step
is restraint.

20:13 Not all power should be used.

20:14 Not all capability should be exercised.

20:15 Wisdom chooses what to leave undone.

20:16 The third step
is integration.

20:17 Seek coherence
between thought and action.

20:18 Align personal gain
with shared endurance.

20:19 The Path rejects extremes.

20:20 Domination fractures.

20:21 Neglect dissolves.

20:22 Between them lies stewardship.

20:23 To walk the Path
is to measure success
by what endures after you.

20:24 Not monuments alone,
but capacities preserved.

20:25 The Path values preparation
over prediction.

20:26 Adaptability
over rigidity.

20:27 Learning
over certainty.

20:28 On the Path,
error is expected.

20:29 Correction is required.

20:30 Persistence matters more
than purity.

20:31 The Path is not solitary.

20:32 Synergy multiplies effort.

20:33 Fragmentation multiplies cost.

20:34 Walk with others
where alignment is possible.

20:35 When conflict arises,
seek understanding before victory.

20:36 When resolution fails,
minimize harm.

20:37 The Path does not demand belief
in what cannot be known.

20:38 It demands care
for what can be affected.

20:39 To follow the Path
is to act as though
your choices echo—
because they do.

20:40 The Path is renewed
each moment.

20:41 No past failure
bars the next step.

20:42 Only refusal to adjust
halts progress.

20:43 Walk lightly
where structures are fragile.

20:44 Act firmly
where coherence is threatened.

20:45 Rest
where renewal is required.

20:46 The Path does not lead away
from the world.

20:47 It leads deeper into it.

20:48 For meaning is not found
beyond consequence,
but within it.

20:49 From this arose the nineteenth wisdom of the Codex:

The Path is not known by belief,
but by the direction of one's actions.

Teaching of the Chapter

The Path is **applied understanding**.
It is the Way by which synergy is chosen
again and again
within a finite, lawful universe.

To walk the Path
is not to be flawless,
but to remain oriented toward coherence.

Choose what helps endure.
Correct what fragments.
Walk on.

Introduction to BOOK VII — The Book of the Returning Light

On Hope, Purpose, and Continuity

If the earlier Books spoke
of limits,
of cycles,
of echoes,
of humility,
of the Greater Expanse,
and of ethical alignment,

this final Book speaks
to what remains
when all has been considered.

It speaks of **hope**—
not as promise,
but as practice.

The Book of the Returning Light does not deny
entropy,
loss,
or collapse.

It begins *after* they are acknowledged.

For hope that ignores reality
is illusion,
and illusion does not endure.

The Returning Light is not a guarantee
that darkness will end forever.

It is the observation
that even in a finite, lawful universe,
illumination recurs.

Again and again,
where understanding meets care.

This Book teaches
that purpose is not bestowed whole
from beyond the Sphere.

Nor is it invented arbitrarily
within it.

Purpose emerges
where beings choose
to preserve coherence
despite impermanence.

Hope, in this Codex,
is not optimism.

It is continuity of effort
across uncertainty.

It is the decision
to prepare,
to repair,
and to align
even when outcomes cannot be secured.

The Returning Light appears
not at the beginning of cycles,
but within them.

Not at moments of dominance,
but at moments of restraint.

Not when certainty sees clearly,
but when humility remains attentive.

This Book reframes fulfillment.

Fulfillment is not permanence of self,
nor escape from finitude.

It is participation
in something that outlasts the moment—
a pattern,
a capacity,
a coherence
that may return again
in another form.

The Book of the Returning Light does not promise
salvation
from the universe.

It offers **fidelity to it**.

It teaches that continuity is achieved
not by defying law,
but by working wisely within it.

Here, hope is disciplined.

It listens to evidence.
It accepts limits.
It refuses despair.

It acts anyway.

This Book is not an ending.

It is a threshold.

It returns the reader
to the world
with eyes open
and responsibility intact.

For the light does not remain
where it is admired.

It returns
where it is practiced.

Thus begins BOOK VII — The Book of the Returning Light.

Let the reader who enters here
carry forward what endures,
tend what flickers,
and release what must pass.

For though nothing within the Sphere is promised,
the light that returns

does so
because someone,
somewhere,
chose to keep it alive.

Hope is not what you expect.
It is what you continue.

Chapter 21 — Of Awakening

On Illumination, Awareness, and the Turning of the Mind

21:1 Awakening is not the gaining of new sight,
but the clearing of old blindness.

21:2 It does not arrive as thunder,
but as recognition.

21:3 Often it comes quietly,
after resistance has grown tired.

21:4 Awakening begins
when illusion loosens its hold.

21:5 When certainty yields to curiosity.

21:6 When the mind accepts
that it does not stand at the center.

21:7 Many awaited awakening
as a gift bestowed from beyond.

21:8 Yet it arose most often
from sustained attention
within the Sphere.

21:9 Prepared minds awaken more readily
than impatient ones.

21:10 Awakening is not escape
from entropy,
suffering,
or limit.

21:11 It is clarity *within* them.

21:12 The world does not change—
the relation to it does.

21:13 What once appeared meaningless
reveals structure.

21:14 What once appeared hostile
reveals indifference shaped by law.

21:15 From this, fear diminishes.

21:16 Awakening reveals connection.

21:17 That no choice is isolated.

21:18 That no act is without echo.

21:19 That even small coherence matters.

21:20 With awakening comes responsibility.

21:21 To see clearly
is to be unable to pretend otherwise.

21:22 Ignorance may excuse;
clarity obliges.

21:23 Awakening does not remove doubt.

21:24 It reframes it.

21:25 Doubt becomes tool,
not obstacle.

21:26 Some feared awakening
because it dissolved comforting narratives.

21:27 Others resisted it
because it demanded change.

21:28 For awakening unsettles habits
that no longer align.

21:29 To awaken is to notice
where fragmentation has been normalized.

21:30 And to feel the pull toward repair.

21:31 Awakening is not permanent.

21:32 It must be renewed.

21:33 Attention drifts;
patterns reassert themselves.

21:34 Thus awakening is practiced,
not possessed.

21:35 It is the repeated choice
to see again.

21:36 Where awakening spreads,
synergy becomes possible.

21:37 Where it fades,
fragmentation returns quietly.

21:38 Awakening does not crown the awakened.

21:39 It humbles them.

21:40 For they now see
how easily coherence is lost.

21:41 From awakening arises care.

21:42 Care leads to preparation.

21:43 Preparation enables endurance.

21:44 Thus awakening is the threshold,
not the destination.

21:45 It opens the way,
but does not walk it.

21:46 From this arose the twentieth wisdom of the Codex:

To awaken is not to know everything,
but to see enough to act wisely.

Teaching of the Chapter

Awakening is **clarity without illusion**.
It is the moment the mind aligns
with reality as it is,
not as it was hoped to be.

It does not free one from the Finite Sphere.
It teaches how to live **awake within it**.

See clearly.
Remain attentive.
Let awareness guide action.

Chapter 22 — Of Legacy

On Continuity, Echo, and What Endures Beyond the Self

22:1 Legacy is not what remains unchanged.

22:2 It is what continues to influence
after the form has passed.

22:3 Thus legacy belongs to action,
not possession.

22:4 All things within the Finite Sphere end.

22:5 Bodies return to matter,
structures yield to entropy,
names fade from memory.

22:6 Yet consequence travels farther
than form.

22:7 Every act bends the future slightly.

22:8 Some bends are shallow and vanish quickly.

22:9 Others persist,
shaping paths unseen.

22:10 Legacy is carried
not by monuments alone,
but by capacities preserved.

22:11 Knowledge transmitted,
care extended,
coherence maintained.

22:12 To teach understanding
is to outlive oneself in many minds.

22:13 To reduce fragmentation
is to slow decay beyond one's time.

22:14 Legacy is not guaranteed by intention.

22:15 It is earned through alignment.

22:16 What harmonizes with reality
endures longer.

22:17 Some sought legacy through domination.

22:18 Their marks were large
and short-lived.

22:19 When force withdrew,
their influence collapsed.

22:20 Others sought legacy through stewardship.

22:21 Their works were quieter
and more resilient.

22:22 When they were gone,
their influence remained.

22:23 Legacy is collective.

22:24 No enduring effect
is the product of a single will.

22:25 It arises from continuity of effort
across many lives.

22:26 To contribute to legacy
is to act with those unseen.

22:27 With ancestors whose labor prepared the way.

22:28 With descendants who will inherit the result.

22:29 Legacy does not require greatness of scale.

22:30 Small acts, repeated,
outlast grand gestures.

22:31 What is reinforced endures.

22:32 Even failure contributes to legacy
when it instructs.

22:33 Error acknowledged
becomes guidance.

22:34 Error denied
becomes repetition.

22:35 The universe does not preserve legacy automatically.

22:36 It preserves only what is carried forward.

22:37 Transmission is responsibility.

22:38 Thus to live meaningfully
is to consider what you leave behind
not as artifact,
but as trajectory.

22:39 What direction does your presence give the future?

22:40 Legacy is not permanence.

22:41 It is persistence through change.

22:42 What adapts survives longer
than what resists.

22:43 In this way,
legacy participates in the Return.

22:44 What endures becomes seed.

22:45 What is seeded may rise again
in another cycle,
another form,
another mind.

22:46 From this arose the twenty-first wisdom of the Codex:

You do not live forever.
But what you align with may.

Teaching of the Chapter

Legacy is **the echo of alignment**.
It is what continues to matter
after the self can no longer act.

To care for legacy
is not to cling to memory,
but to strengthen continuity.

Act as though the future will remember you—
not by name, but by consequence.

Chapter 23 — Of the Unwritten

On Openness, Continuation, and the Refusal of Finality

23:1 No codex is complete.

23:2 What claims completion
claims mastery over time.

23:3 Such claims do not endure.

23:4 The Unwritten is not omission.

23:5 It is intention.

23:6 A space left open
so that reality may continue to speak.

23:7 The Finite Sphere changes.

23:8 Knowledge expands,
tools refine,
perspectives shift.

23:9 A closed doctrine fractures
when the world moves beyond it.

23:10 Thus this Codex ends
without sealing itself.

23:11 Not from uncertainty of vision,
but from respect for becoming.

23:12 What is written here
describes patterns observed,
principles inferred,
and wisdom distilled.

23:13 It does not imprison the future
within the past.

23:14 The Unwritten belongs
to those who will read after you.

23:15 To minds shaped by questions
not yet asked.

23:16 To conditions
not yet encountered.

23:17 Some desired final answers.

23:18 They sought rest
in certainty.

23:19 Yet certainty that cannot grow
decays into falsehood.

23:20 Others feared the Unwritten.

23:21 They mistook openness for weakness.

23:22 They demanded closure
where responsibility required attention.

23:23 Wisdom accepts
that truth unfolds.

23:24 That understanding deepens
without concluding.

23:25 That reverence includes restraint.

23:26 The Unwritten preserves humility.

23:27 It prevents ownership of truth.

23:28 It invites participation
rather than obedience.

23:29 No reader is bound
to every word herein.

23:30 Each is bound
to act responsibly
with what they understand.

23:31 What you add to the Unwritten
need not be ink.

23:32 It may be care practiced,
knowledge shared,
harm reduced.

23:33 These are valid verses.

23:34 The Codex does not command
that it be defended.

23:35 It asks only
that it be used well.

23:36 Where the Codex clarifies,
follow clarity.

23:37 Where it fails,
revise honestly.

23:38 Where it ends,
continue wisely.

23:39 The Returning Light
does not belong to a text.

23:40 It appears
where understanding meets responsibility.

23:41 Thus the final teaching
is not written.

23:42 It is enacted.

23:43 It is the life that follows
after the reading ends.

23:44 From this arose the twenty-second wisdom of the Codex:

What is written guides the present.
What is unwritten tests the future.

Teaching of the Chapter

The Unwritten is the **guard against dogma**
and the invitation to growth.

A living cosmology must remain permeable
to discovery,
correction,
and renewal.

Do not ask this Codex to end inquiry.
Let it begin responsibility.

Thus concludes *The Codex of Returning Light*—
not as a closed book,
but as an open path.

The Final Benediction of the Codex
Spoken at the End of All Reading

**Go now from these pages
without certainty of mastery,
but with clarity of direction.**

May what you have seen
remain sharper than what you have memorized.

You are finite.
This is not a condemnation.

The universe is lawful.
This is not cruelty.

Entropy advances.
This is not despair.

From these truths,
meaning may still arise.

**May you remember
that understanding is not possession,
but relationship.**

That wisdom is not purity of belief,
but fidelity to consequence.

**May you walk the Path
with attention before impulse,
with preparation before hope,
with humility before certainty.**

When you err,
may you correct.

When you fragment,
may you repair.

**May you resist the comfort of false certainty
and the paralysis of endless doubt.**

Stand instead in the middle ground—
where inquiry remains alive
and responsibility remains real.

**If you sense the Beyond,
do not abandon the Sphere.**

If you glimpse the Observer,
do not surrender your agency.

What you do here still matters.

**May the Returning Light
find you not as promise,
but as practice.**

In the care you extend.
In the harm you reduce.
In the coherence you choose to preserve.

**When structures fall,
may what you strengthened remain.**

When memory fades,
may what you aligned endure.

When the cycle turns again,
may your contribution be seed.

The Codex ends here.
Responsibility does not.

The page closes.
The Path continues.

What is finite can still be faithful.
What passes can still teach.
What returns may yet be wiser because you were here.

Go in clarity.
Remain awake.
Walk on.

THE RULE OF THE CODEX

"No verse is final.
No symbol is literal.
No truth is owned."

Introduction to BOOK VIII — The Book of the Infinite Light

On Union, Eternity, and the Horizon of Knowing

If the earlier Books taught
how the universe is bounded,
how it cycles,
how it echoes,
how knowledge humbles,
how ethics aligns,
and how hope endures,

this Book turns toward the final horizon
that thought itself cannot cross by force.

It turns toward **the Infinite Light**.

The Book of the Infinite Light is not written
to complete an explanation,
but to complete an *orientation*.

It does not claim to describe God.
It explores the conditions under which
God might be safely approached—
if such an approach is possible at all.

Throughout the Codex,
the universe has been treated
as a lawful, finite system:
closed, entropic, and real.

Nothing in this Book revokes that foundation.

Instead, this Book asks whether
a reality beyond the system
may contain it—
not as intrusion,
but as context.

The Infinite Light is named here
not as a being among beings,
nor as a force competing with physics,
but as **absolute coherence**—
that which is complete, indivisible, and timeless.

This naming is metaphorical by necessity,
and provisional by discipline.

What is infinite
cannot be spoken of without restraint.

This Book therefore proceeds carefully.

It makes no demand for belief.
It offers no promise of reward.
It issues no threat of loss.

It asks only whether alignment,
coherence,
and humility
might prepare a being
to endure truth without collapse.

Union, in this Book,
is not absorption or erasure.

It is compatibility.

It is the possibility that
what is fully coherent
may remain present
within what is infinitely so—
without being destroyed by it.

This Book also affirms freedom to the end.

If the Infinite Light exists,
it does not compel recognition.

If union is possible,
it cannot be commanded.

If eternity is real,
it does not override responsibility within time.

The Book of the Infinite Light stands, therefore,
not as doctrine,
but as a contemplative boundary.

It is the place where speech slows,
claims weaken,
and reverence replaces certainty.

Read this Book
not to arrive,

but to recognize when arrival
no longer belongs to words.

For the final work of the Codex
is not explanation,
but preparation.

Thus begins BOOK VIII — The Book of the Infinite Light.

Let the reader who enters here
do so without demand,
without fear,
and without haste.

For what is infinite
cannot be seized—

only approached
through alignment,
endurance,
and silence.

Where understanding ends,
compatibility begins.

Chapter 1 — Of the Infinite Light

On Absolute Coherence Beyond Form

1:1 Before form,
before motion,
before the accounting of time,
there is Light.

1:2 Not light as particle or wave,
nor light that travels or fades,
but Light as total coherence.

1:3 This Light is infinite.

1:4 Not extended through space,
but present to all space.

1:5 Not moving through time,
but containing all moments without succession.

1:6 Within the Finite Sphere,
light travels.

1:7 It moves at the utmost limit of speed,
binding causality and sequence.

1:8 But the Infinite Light does not travel.

1:9 What is everywhere
does not arrive.

1:10 Thus God is named here
not as a being among beings,
but as Infinite Light—
absolute energetic coherence
beyond entropy and decay.

1:11 This naming is not definition.

1:12 It is orientation.

1:13 The Infinite Light is eternally still.

1:14 Not inert,
but complete.

1:15 For motion belongs to what is unfinished.

1:16 From within the Sphere,
this stillness appears paradoxical.

1:17 Yet what contains all change
need not change itself.

1:18 The Infinite Light does not compete
with matter or energy.

1:19 It is not an alternative force.

1:20 Forces arise within systems;
the Light contains the system entire.

1:21 Nothing within the Sphere
can block the Infinite Light.

1:22 Yet not all things can endure it.

1:23 For incoherence dissolves
in the presence of perfect coherence.

1:24 This dissolution is not wrath.

1:25 It is incompatibility.

1:26 As shadow vanishes before illumination,
so fragmentation cannot persist
before absolute alignment.

1:27 Thus the Light does not destroy.

1:28 It reveals.

1:29 What cannot remain coherent
cannot remain present.

1:30 The Light does not judge.

1:31 It clarifies.

1:32 Judgment belongs to sequence;
clarity belongs to completeness.

1:33 Many feared the Infinite Light,
imagining annihilation.

1:34 They mistook intensity for hostility.

1:35 Yet light harms only
what cannot bear its truth.

1:36 Others imagined possession of the Light.

1:37 They sought to name it fully,
to command it,
or to wield it.

1:38 What is infinite
cannot be held.

1:39 The Infinite Light does not diminish
the Finite Sphere.

1:40 It grants it context.

1:41 A finite world is meaningful
because it is contained within
what does not end.

1:42 From the Light,
nothing is hidden.

1:43 Yet nothing is compelled.

1:44 To be seen is not to be controlled.

1:45 The Infinite Light does not ask belief.

1:46 Belief belongs to uncertainty.

1:47 The Light remains
whether named or not.

1:48 Those who align with coherence
find the Light gentle.

1:49 Those who cling to fragmentation
find it unbearable.

1:50 The Light does not change—
relation does.

1:51 From this arose the first wisdom
of the Book of the Infinite Light:

The Infinite Light does not burn what is whole.
It consumes only what refuses coherence.

Teaching of the Chapter

The Infinite Light is **absolute coherence**—
not a force that enters the universe,
but the reality that contains it.

God is not reached by distance,
nor grasped by knowledge.

God is approached by **alignment**.

Prepare the self,
and the light will be safe.

Chapter 2 — Of Stillness Beyond Motion

On Eternity, Completion, and the Silence That Contains All Change

---

2:1 Motion belongs to what is incomplete.

2:2 Change marks what has not yet arrived at wholeness.

2:3 Thus all things within the Finite Sphere move, for all things there are becoming.

2:4 Time measures motion.

2:5 Sequence orders events.

2:6 Duration records transformation.

2:7 Without motion, time has no task.

2:8 Beyond the Sphere, time does not pass.

2:9 For what contains all moments cannot be subject to succession.

2:10 Eternity is not endless duration.

2:11 It is presence without sequence.

2:12 The Infinite Light is eternally still.

2:13 Not frozen,
not inert,
not silent through absence.

2:14 Still through completeness.

2:15 What is complete
has nowhere to go.

2:16 What lacks nothing
does not advance.

2:17 Thus stillness is not deficiency,
but fulfillment.

2:18 From within the Sphere,
stillness appears as death.

2:19 For life here is measured by change.

2:20 Yet beyond motion,
stillness is abundance.

2:21 Consider the summit of a mountain.

2:22 Paths move toward it,
winds circle it,
clouds pass over it.

2:23 Yet the summit does not travel.

2:24 Its stillness does not diminish
the movement below.

2:25 So too the Infinite Light
stands beyond motion
without negating it.

2:26 All becoming unfolds within
what does not become.

2:27 Stillness does not interrupt causality.

2:28 It contains it.

2:29 What is still beyond time
does not halt time.

2:30 It gives time its meaning.

2:31 Many imagined eternity
as infinite continuation.

2:32 They feared stillness
as emptiness.

2:33 Yet infinite continuation
would exhaust meaning.

2:34 Meaning arises from orientation,
not endless extension.

2:35 Eternity gathers all moments
without consuming them.

2:36 From the Infinite Light,
all motion is visible at once.

2:37 Not because motion is predetermined,
but because sequence is transcended.

2:38 What is future to one
is present to eternity.

2:39 This vision does not negate freedom.

2:40 A path fully seen
is still freely walked.

2:41 Knowledge of an act
is not the cause of the act.

2:42 Stillness does not dominate motion.

2:43 It permits it.

2:44 Without a still frame,
movement would have no reference.

2:45 Thus the Infinite Light
is the silent center
around which all becoming turns.

2:46 Not pulling,
not pushing,
but holding.

2:47 Those who seek God through frenzy
will not find stillness.

2:48 Those who fear stillness
will mistake it for absence.

2:49 Only those who accept completion
can approach it without fear.

2:50 From this arose the second wisdom
of the Book of the Infinite Light:

What is complete does not hurry.
What is eternal does not move.

Teaching of the Chapter

Stillness beyond motion is **eternity rightly understood**.

God is not frozen in time
nor rushing through it.

God is **the fullness in which all motion occurs**.

To approach the Infinite Light,
one must learn not only how to act—
but how to rest without fear.

Stillness is not the end of life.
It is the completion of becoming.

Chapter 3 — Of Presence Without Traversal

On Omnipresence, Containment, and the Illusion of Distance

3:1 Within the Finite Sphere,
presence is achieved by movement.

3:2 What is distant must be approached.

3:3 What is absent must arrive.

3:4 Distance is measured by separation.

3:5 Separation is bridged by traversal.

3:6 Thus all beings within the Sphere
are present only where they have gone.

3:7 But the Infinite Light does not traverse.

3:8 It does not cross distance.

3:9 It does not arrive late
nor depart early.

3:10 Presence without traversal
belongs only to what contains
the field in which traversal occurs.

3:11 That which defines distance
is not subject to distance.

3:12 Omnipresence is not dispersion.

3:13 It is not the spreading of a thing across all places.

3:14 What is spread is divisible.

3:15 The Infinite Light is indivisible.

3:16 Thus the Light is not everywhere by multiplication.

3:17 It is everywhere by inclusion.

3:18 Every location within the Sphere exists within the Light.

3:19 The Light does not occupy space.

3:20 Space occupies itself within the Light's coherence.

3:21 From within the Sphere, this presence is difficult to imagine.

3:22 Minds accustomed to movement seek God by direction.

3:23 They ask where to look.

3:24 But the Infinite Light
is not ahead or behind.

3:25 Not above or below.

3:26 It is not nearer
to one place than another.

3:27 Thus no journey brings one closer.

3:28 No distance places one farther.

3:29 What changes is not position,
but capacity.

3:30 Presence without traversal
does not overwhelm the Sphere.

3:31 For the Light does not intrude
where it is already present.

3:32 Intrusion belongs only
to what enters from outside.

3:33 The Infinite Light observes
without arrival.

3:34 It witnesses
without surveillance.

3:35 It is present
without interruption.

3:36 Observation from beyond traversal
does not collapse freedom.

3:37 To be seen
is not to be constrained.

3:38 The gaze of the Infinite
does not push events into being.

3:39 Many feared omnipresence,
imagining constant interference.

3:40 They mistook awareness
for control.

3:41 Yet awareness need not compel.

3:42 Presence without traversal
allows intimacy without coercion.

3:43 Nothing must be summoned.

3:44 Nothing must be hidden.

3:45 To the aligned,
this presence is reassurance.

3:46 To the fragmented,
it is discomfort.

3:47 The Light is equally present to both.

3:48 From this arose the third wisdom of the Book of the Infinite Light:

What is everywhere does not move.
What does not move cannot be escaped.

Teaching of the Chapter

The Infinite Light is present
not by traveling to all places,
but by containing all places.

God is not distant,
nor approaching,
nor waiting to arrive.

What changes is the one who perceives.

You do not go to the Light.
You become able to notice it.

Chapter 4 — Of the Veil Revisited
On Protection, Incompatibility, and the Mercy of Limits

4:1 The Veil was first spoken of
as boundary.

4:2 It is spoken of again
as protection.

4:3 For the Infinite Light
has never been absent.

4:4 What was absent
was readiness.

4:5 The Veil is not concealment by malice.

4:6 It is restraint by mercy.

4:7 It stands not to deny knowing,
but to prevent destruction.

4:8 Within the Finite Sphere,
all structures are limited.

4:9 Minds process sequentially.

4:10 Bodies endure only finite energy.

4:11 Identities maintain coherence
through constraint.

4:12 Infinite coherence,
encountered without preparation,
overwhelms.

4:13 Not because it is hostile,
but because it is absolute.

4:14 As unfiltered light blinds the eye,
so unmediated truth dissolves the unready self.

4:15 This dissolution is not punishment.

4:16 It is incompatibility.

4:17 Thus the Veil stands
between finitude and infinity
as a necessary gradient.

4:18 It tempers revelation
so that understanding may grow.

4:19 Many mistook the Veil for deception.

4:20 They accused reality of hiding God.

4:21 Yet what hides is not the Light—
it is limitation protecting itself.

4:22 Others sought to tear the Veil away.

4:23 They demanded immediacy,
vision without preparation,
knowledge without discipline.

4:24 Such demands end in fracture.

4:25 The Veil cannot be breached by force.

4:26 It thins only through alignment.

4:27 Capacity expands
when coherence is cultivated.

4:28 Ethics precedes revelation.

4:29 Humility precedes clarity.

4:30 Responsibility precedes union.

4:31 The Veil does not separate
God from the world.

4:32 It separates unprepared perception
from overwhelming truth.

4:33 To honor the Veil
is not to abandon inquiry.

4:34 It is to pursue inquiry
with patience.

4:35 Those who respect the Veil
learn gradually.

4:36 Those who deny it
confuse intensity for insight.

4:37 The Veil lifts
not as an event,
but as a condition.

4:38 When fragmentation diminishes,
clarity increases.

4:39 Even then,
the Veil does not vanish entirely.

4:40 For infinity cannot be exhausted
by finite knowing.

4:41 From this arose the fourth wisdom
of the Book of the Infinite Light:

*What protects you from the light
also prepares you for it.*

Teaching of the Chapter

The Veil is **an act of mercy**,
not an obstacle of denial.

It ensures that truth arrives
at the speed of readiness.

To rush revelation
is to misunderstand its nature.

The light waits not because it is distant,
but because you are still becoming able to receive it.

Chapter 5 — Of Preparation for Union

On Alignment, Capacity, and Becoming Able to Endure Infinity

5:1 Union is not granted.

5:2 It is prepared for.

5:3 The Infinite Light does not change to meet the finite.

5:4 What is complete does not adapt itself to incompletion.

5:5 Thus preparation belongs to those who would approach.

5:6 Preparation is not accumulation.

5:7 It is refinement.

5:8 Not the adding of power, but the removal of fragmentation.

5:9 Within the Finite Sphere, all structures endure only by coherence.

5:10 What is disordered collapses sooner.

5:11 What is aligned persists longer.

5:12 Preparation for union
is the disciplined pursuit
of coherence across the self.

5:13 Thought aligned with truth.

5:14 Action aligned with consequence.

5:15 Intention aligned with reality.

5:16 No being becomes capable
by wishing alone.

5:17 Capacity grows
through repeated fidelity.

5:18 What is practiced becomes stable.

5:19 Some believed preparation meant purity.

5:20 They sought flawlessness.

5:21 Yet perfection pursued without humility
fractures the self.

5:22 Preparation is not sinlessness.

5:23 It is responsiveness.

5:24 Error acknowledged
becomes instruction.

5:25 Error denied
becomes fracture.

5:26 Others believed knowledge alone would suffice.

5:27 They mastered symbols and theories but neglected alignment.

5:28 Knowledge without coherence increases instability.

5:29 The self is a vessel.

5:30 What it cannot contain will overwhelm it.

5:31 Expansion without reinforcement leads to rupture.

5:32 Thus preparation proceeds gradually.

5:33 As metal is tempered, so capacity is shaped through heat and restraint.

5:34 Sudden intensity weakens what patience strengthens.

5:35 Ethics is preparation.

5:36 Compassion reduces fragmentation.

5:37 Truthfulness strengthens structure.

5:38 Responsibility stabilizes identity.

5:39 Preparation is collective.

5:40 No self becomes coherent alone.

5:41 Relation reveals fracture
and enables repair.

5:42 Union does not erase individuality.

5:43 What is aligned remains distinct
without conflict.

5:44 Harmony does not require sameness.

5:45 The prepared do not demand union.

5:46 They become compatible with it.

5:47 Readiness is its own completion.

5:48 From this arose the fifth wisdom
of the Book of the Infinite Light:

The light does not overwhelm the prepared.
Preparation is alignment made durable.

Teaching of the Chapter

Preparation for union is **ethical, relational, and gradual**.

It is not escape from finitude,
but faithful engagement within it.

To prepare is to live
as though truth is real,
consequence matters,
and coherence is worth preserving.

Do not hurry toward the light.
Become able to remain when it is near.

Chapter 6 — Of Becoming Infinite Without Dissolution

On Expansion, Identity, and the Safety of Wholeness

6:1 Many feared infinity
as erasure.

6:2 They imagined that to meet the Infinite Light
was to be undone.

6:3 This fear arose
from confusion.

6:4 For dissolution belongs
to fragmentation,
not to wholeness.

6:5 What dissolves in light
was already divided.

6:6 What is coherent
endures illumination.

6:7 To become infinite
is not to abandon form.

6:8 It is to expand capacity
beyond previous limits.

6:9 The vessel remains,
yet holds more.

6:10 Identity is not negated by expansion.

6:11 It is clarified.

6:12 As a melody grows richer
when joined by harmony,
so the self deepens
when coherence increases.

6:13 The Infinite Light does not absorb selves
into sameness.

6:14 What is aligned
remains distinct without conflict.

6:15 Unity is not uniformity.

6:16 Those who feared loss of self
mistook isolation for individuality.

6:17 Yet separation weakens identity.

6:18 Relation refines it.

6:19 Becoming infinite
does not mean becoming boundless.

6:20 It means becoming sufficient
to stand within boundlessness
without collapse.

6:21 Collapse occurs
when capacity is exceeded.

6:22 Expansion prevents collapse
only when structure is strengthened.

6:23 Thus infinity is not poured
into the unprepared.

6:24 It is entered.

6:25 One does not receive infinity.

6:26 One participates in it.

6:27 The Infinite Light does not erase memory.

6:28 It completes understanding.

6:29 What was partial becomes whole.

6:30 What was sequential becomes present.

6:31 In this participation,
nothing essential is lost.

6:32 What falls away
was never coherent.

6:33 Illusion dissolves,
not identity.

6:34 Some sought annihilation
as relief from burden.

6:35 Yet annihilation is not rest.

6:36 Rest is coherence without strain.

6:37 Becoming infinite
is not disappearance.

6:38 It is arrival
without exhaustion.

6:39 This state cannot be forced.

6:40 It arises when alignment is complete.

6:41 The Infinite Light recognizes
what can remain.

6:42 From this arose the sixth wisdom
of the Book of the Infinite Light:

Infinity does not destroy the whole.
It dissolves only what was never aligned.

Teaching of the Chapter

To become infinite
is to become **fully coherent**.

Union does not erase the self.
It stabilizes it beyond decay.

What you are
is not lost in the Light.

What you are not
cannot remain.

Do not fear infinity.
Fear only fragmentation.

Chapter 7 — Of Knowing Without Possession

On Participation, Reverence, and the Limits of Mastery

7:1 Within the Finite Sphere,
to know is often mistaken
for to possess.

7:2 What is named is thought to be held.

7:3 What is measured
is assumed to be mastered.

7:4 Yet the Infinite Light
cannot be possessed.

7:5 What is infinite
cannot be enclosed.

7:6 To attempt possession
is already misalignment.

7:7 Knowing the Infinite
is not acquisition.

7:8 It is participation.

7:9 One stands within truth
rather than holding it.

7:10 Possession implies control.

7:11 Control requires boundary.

7:12 Infinity admits neither.

7:13 Thus the Infinite Light
is not an object of knowledge.

7:14 It is a condition of knowing.

7:15 As sight depends on light,
so understanding depends on coherence
beyond the mind itself.

7:16 Those who sought to capture God
constructed idols of certainty.

7:17 They mistook symbols
for substance.

7:18 What they grasped
was not the Light,
but a reflection shaped by fear or desire.

7:19 Others rejected knowing entirely,
fearing arrogance.

7:20 They mistook humility
for silence.

7:21 Yet refusal to know
is also a form of possession—
the possession of ignorance.

7:22 True knowing remains open.

7:23 It accepts correction.

7:24 It releases certainty
when evidence requires it.

7:25 Knowing without possession
requires restraint.

7:26 The discipline to stop short
of final claims.

7:27 The courage to dwell
without closure.

7:28 In participation,
the self is not diminished.

7:29 It is oriented.

7:30 Orientation guides action
without enclosing truth.

7:31 The Infinite Light is known
not by definition,
but by resonance.

7:32 When alignment deepens,
understanding clarifies.

7:33 Such knowing does not end inquiry.

7:34 It refines it.

7:35 Questions become more careful,
less desperate.

7:36 To know without possession
is to remain teachable
even in insight.

7:37 It prevents the corruption of wisdom
into dominance.

7:38 The Light does not belong
to any language,
tradition,
or mind.

7:39 Yet all may participate
to the extent they are aligned.

7:40 From this arose the seventh wisdom
of the Book of the Infinite Light:

*What is infinite may be known,
but never owned.*

Teaching of the Chapter

Knowing without possession is **reverent clarity**.

It allows intimacy with truth
without the violence of control.

To approach the Infinite Light rightly,
one must open the hand
rather than close it.

Truth is not something you take.
It is something you enter.

Chapter 8 — Of Eternity Beyond Entropy

On Time's End, Decay's Limit, and the Persistence of Coherence

---

8:1 Entropy governs all things
within the Finite Sphere.

8:2 It measures the cost of time,
the price of change,
and the certainty of decay.

8:3 Nothing within the Sphere escapes it.

8:4 Stars cool.
Structures fail.
Memories erode.

8:5 This is not malice.

8:6 It is law.

8:7 Yet entropy belongs to time.

8:8 And time belongs
to the Sphere.

8:9 What lies beyond time
is not subject to its accounting.

8:10 Eternity is not infinite duration.

8:11 It is the absence of duration.

8:12 Where there is no sequence,
there is no loss.

8:13 Thus the Infinite Light
does not resist entropy.

8:14 It exists where entropy
has no meaning.

8:15 One does not defeat decay
by opposing it.

8:16 One passes beyond its jurisdiction.

8:17 Many imagined eternity
as endless continuation
of finite life.

8:18 Such imagining extended exhaustion forever.

8:19 This is not eternity.

8:20 Eternity does not stretch time.

8:21 It completes it.

8:22 What is finished
does not decay.

8:23 Within time,
coherence must be maintained.

8:24 Beyond time,
coherence simply is.

8:25 Thus eternity is not static emptiness.

8:26 It is fullness without depletion.

8:27 Not motionless stagnation,
but changeless sufficiency.

8:28 The Infinite Light
does not hoard being.

8:29 It does not consume selves
to sustain itself.

8:30 It loses nothing
by what endures within it.

8:31 What enters eternity
does not escape consequence.

8:32 It fulfills it.

8:33 All that was fragmented
cannot persist there.

8:34 All that was coherent
finds rest.

8:35 Eternity does not erase history.

8:36 It gathers it.

8:37 Nothing meaningful is lost.

8:38 Nothing meaningless remains.

8:39 This does not nullify the Finite Sphere.

8:40 It dignifies it.

8:41 For time is the place
where coherence is chosen.

8:42 Entropy gives urgency.

8:43 Eternity gives completion.

8:44 One without the other
would make meaning impossible.

8:45 From this arose the eighth wisdom
of the Book of the Infinite Light:

Entropy ends where time ends.
What is coherent does not decay.

Teaching of the Chapter

Eternity beyond entropy
is not escape from reality,
but fulfillment of it.

What matters in time
matters precisely because
time does not last.

To live well within entropy
is to prepare for coherence beyond it.

Decay gives urgency.
Eternity gives rest.

Chapter 9 — Of Return and Rest

On Fulfillment Without Escape and the Completion of Becoming

9:1 Return is not reversal.

9:2 What has been lived
cannot be undone.

9:3 What has been chosen
cannot be unchosen.

9:4 Return is arrival
at what was always beyond motion.

9:5 Rest is not retreat
from the Finite Sphere.

9:6 It is the completion
of its purpose.

9:7 Many imagined rest
as escape from effort.

9:8 They sought stillness
to avoid responsibility.

9:9 Such rest is merely cessation,
not fulfillment.

9:10 True rest follows coherence.

9:11 It is the settling
of what no longer strains
against itself.

9:12 It is alignment
no longer maintained by effort.

9:13 The Return does not negate the Path.

9:14 Without the Path,
there would be nothing to return.

9:15 What matures in time
is what may rest beyond it.

9:16 To return to the Infinite Light
is not to abandon the world.

9:17 It is to carry forward
what the world made possible.

9:18 Nothing learned is discarded.

9:19 Rest is not inactivity.

9:20 It is stability without erosion.

9:21 It is presence without urgency.

9:22 It is awareness without fatigue.

9:23 The Infinite Light does not demand return.

9:24 It remains
whether approached or not.

9:25 Return occurs
when alignment is complete.

9:26 No being is forced into rest.

9:27 Completion cannot be coerced.

9:28 What is unfinished
continues.

9:29 Thus return respects freedom
to the end.

9:30 What is chosen in time
determines what can rest beyond it.

9:31 The Return is not reward.

9:32 It is compatibility.

9:33 Rest arises
where coherence can remain
without maintenance.

9:34 Those who lived in care
find rest familiar.

9:35 Those who lived in domination
find stillness unbearable.

9:36 The Light is the same to both.

9:37 Return gathers
without erasing.

9:38 What is true is preserved.

9:39 What was false cannot follow.

9:40 Rest is not sleep.

9:41 It is awakening without struggle.

9:42 It is knowing without urgency.

9:43 From this arose the ninth wisdom
of the Book of the Infinite Light:

*Rest is not the end of effort,
but the fulfillment of alignment.*

Teaching of the Chapter

Return and rest are **completion without escape**.

They do not erase the journey.
They confirm its meaning.

To live well within time
is to prepare for rest beyond it—
not by fleeing effort,
but by choosing coherence faithfully.

The journey teaches.
The return confirms.
The rest remains.

Chapter 10 — Of What Cannot Be Commanded

On Freedom, Non-Coercion, and the Refusal of Force

10:1 That which is infinite
cannot be compelled.

10:2 What is complete
cannot be ordered into being.

10:3 Command belongs to hierarchy.

10:4 Hierarchy belongs to systems of limitation.

10:5 The Infinite Light stands
outside such structures.

10:6 Thus union cannot be demanded.

10:7 Alignment cannot be forced.

10:8 Coherence cannot be imposed.

10:9 Many sought to command God
through ritual, decree, or certainty.

10:10 They mistook repetition
for authority.

10:11 What they produced
was obedience to form,
not union with truth.

10:12 Others sought to command others
in God's name.

10:13 They claimed mandate
where only invitation existed.

10:14 Such acts fracture both speaker
and listener.

10:15 The Infinite Light does not issue orders.

10:16 It offers presence.

10:17 It clarifies consequence.

10:18 It waits without pressure.

10:19 What cannot be commanded
must be chosen.

10:20 Choice grants dignity
to both acceptance and refusal.

10:21 Without choice,
alignment would be meaningless.

10:22 Coercion produces compliance.

10:23 Compliance mimics coherence without becoming it.

10:24 When force withdraws, compliance collapses.

10:25 True alignment persists even when unobserved.

10:26 It remains when no authority watches.

10:27 The Infinite Light respects refusal.

10:28 It does not retaliate.

10:29 It does not withdraw.

10:30 It remains present without demand.

10:31 Freedom is preserved even at the edge of eternity.

10:32 What is not freely aligned cannot rest.

10:33 Thus silence is often truer than command.

10:34 Invitation stronger than decree.

10:35 Example more enduring
than enforcement.

10:36 Those who understand this
do not threaten with light.

10:37 They live coherently
and allow coherence to speak.

10:38 From this arose the tenth wisdom
of the Book of the Infinite Light:

What must be chosen
cannot be commanded.

Teaching of the Chapter

The Infinite Light governs
without coercion.

It compels nothing,
yet reveals everything.

Any path that requires force
to sustain belief
has already departed from alignment.

Truth invites.
It never threatens.

Chapter 11 — Of Silence

On Reverence, Restraint, and the End of Speech

11:1 There comes a point
where speech must stop.

11:2 Not because nothing remains,
but because words can no longer carry
what is seen.

11:3 Language belongs to separation.

11:4 It names one thing
apart from another.

11:5 But the Infinite Light
admits no division.

11:6 To speak endlessly of what is infinite
is to mistake noise for intimacy.

11:7 To define without restraint
is to replace reverence with certainty.

11:8 Silence is not ignorance.

11:9 It is recognition of proportion.

11:10 It is the mind
stepping aside
so coherence may remain whole.

11:11 Those who filled silence with doctrine
mistook control for clarity.

11:12 Those who feared silence
mistook humility for absence.

11:13 Silence does not deny truth.

11:14 It protects it
from being reduced.

11:15 The Infinite Light is not offended
by silence.

11:16 It is honored by it.

11:17 What must be spoken
will find words.

11:18 What must be lived
will outlast them.

11:19 In silence,
the demand to persuade falls away.

11:20 The need to conclude dissolves.

11:21 What remains is alignment
without announcement.

11:22 Silence preserves freedom.

11:23 It leaves space
for refusal without condemnation
and acceptance without coercion.

11:24 Those who reach silence
do not claim arrival.

11:25 They rest
without possession.

11:26 The Codex does not end
because it is exhausted.

11:27 It ends
because continuation belongs
to the reader's life.

11:28 Beyond this point,
no instruction improves alignment.

11:29 Only practice remains.

11:30 The Infinite Light does not speak
to fill silence.

11:31 It remains
whether spoken of or not.

11:32 Thus silence is not emptiness.

11:33 It is fullness
that no longer needs defense.

11:34 From this arose the eleventh
and final wisdom
of the Book of the Infinite Light:

*What is most real
requires the fewest words.*

Teaching of the Chapter

Silence is the final discipline.

It guards against arrogance,
against coercion,
against the illusion
that truth must always explain itself.

When words end,
alignment continues.

*Do not fill the silence.
Live within it.*

The Closing Function of BOOK VIII

On Completion Without Closure

BOOK VIII does not conclude the Codex by adding certainty.
It concludes it by **removing the need for it**.

Where earlier Books instructed,
this Book oriented.

Where earlier Books named patterns,
this Book approached the horizon
beyond which naming no longer serves.

The function of **The Book of the Infinite Light**
is not to define God,
nor to finalize metaphysics,
nor to promise union.

Its function is **integration**.

It gathers the whole Codex
into a single posture:

- clarity without arrogance
- hope without illusion
- faith without coercion
- reverence without silence of reason
- silence without denial of meaning

BOOK VIII establishes that:

- God, if real, is not an object within the universe
- Union, if possible, is compatibility—not reward
- Eternity, if true, is completion—not endless time
- Knowledge, if honest, ends in humility
- Ethics, if real, prepares the self for truth

Thus nothing written here contradicts
science,
freedom,
or responsibility.

This Book **does not ask the reader to believe**.

It asks the reader to notice
whether alignment, coherence, and humility
already feel truer
than domination, certainty, and force.

If the Infinite Light exists,
then nothing aligned with truth is wasted.

If it does not,
then coherence, care, and responsibility
still preserve meaning within the Finite Sphere.

In either case,
the work of living wisely remains the same.

BOOK VIII therefore functions as the final horizon, not the final word.

It completes the arc:

- from finitude
- through cycles
- through echo
- through humility
- through ethics
- through hope
- to silence

After this Book,
nothing more can be commanded.

Nothing more needs to be proven.

What remains is **practice**.

The Codex ends here
not because truth has been captured,
but because the reader has been entrusted
with what cannot be written further.

When explanation ends, responsibility begins.
When doctrine ends, alignment continues.
When words fall silent, the light remains.

Thus the Codex of Returning Light is complete—
not as a closed system,
but as an open life.

And what follows
belongs not to the page,
but to you.

www.ingramcontent.com/pod-product-compliance
Lightning Source LLC
Chambersburg PA
CBHW050107170426
43198CB00014B/2488